Mountains to Sound
GREENWAY

Hiking the
Mountains to Sound
GREENWAY

Harvey Manning

Photos by Bob and Ira Spring

The Mountaineers

Published by The Mountaineers
1011 SW Klickitat Way, Seattle, Washington 98134

Published simultaneously in Canada by Douglas & McIntyre, Ltd., 1615 Venables Street, Vancouver, B.C. V5L 2H1

Published simultaneously in Great Britain by Cordee, 3a DeMontfort Street, Leicester, England, LE1 7HD

Manufactured in the United States of America
Edited by Dana Fos
Maps by Gary Rands
All photographs by Bob and Ira Spring, except those by Ted Thompson on pages 171 and 179
Cover design by Lynne Faulk
Book design, layout, and typesetting by The Mountaineers Books

Cover photograph: Middle fork Snoqualmie River and Mount Garfield
Frontispiece: Mount Garfield from Quartz Creek Road, a spur of the Taylor River Road

Library of Congress Cataloging-in-Publication Data
Manning, Harvey.
    Hiking the Mountains to Sound Greenway /
Harvey Manning ; photos by Bob and Ira Spring.
       p.   cm.
    Includes index.
    ISBN 0-89886-369-4
    1. Hiking--Washington (State)--Puget Sound Region--Guidebooks.
2. Hiking--Interstate 90 Region--Guidebooks. 3. Puget Sound Region (Wash.)--Guidebooks. 4. Interstate 90--Guidebooks. I. Title.
GV199.42.W22P836   1993
796.5'1'0916432--dc20   93-6011
                                    CIP

Contents

Acknowledgments

The Chief Surveyor and his trusty Assistant Surveyor (who packs the cameras around, usually on the back of *his* Assistant) wish to thank the field agents who contributed information about trails and in some cases built them.

Pat Brewington, president of Snoqualmie Valley Trails Club, reviewed the entire manuscript, corrected and added data, counseled on delicate matters of community relations and politics, and philosophized on the prospects for pedestrianism in the area for which her club is the Designated Defender.

Ted Thomsen, board member and secretary of the Mountains to Sound Greenway Trust and a director of the Issaquah Alps Trails Club, reviewed the manuscript on behalf of these two organizations and provided wise counsel about trails and good advice on the ways of the world outside trail country.

Before and after the 1990 Mountains to Sound March, the Rattlesnake Rangers, volunteers drawn mainly from the two trails clubs, thoroughly tramped the ups and downs of their favorite Alp. They then volunteered to write up their bootways: the Rattlesnake Mountain section in this book is almost entirely their work.

Other explorers made significant contributions by telephone, letter, and pieces written for *Signpost Magazine* and *Pack and Paddle*. They are acknowledged in the trip descriptions that draw on their help.

I-90 freeway from Iron Horse Trail

Introduction

The Vision

To drive from Seattle to Ellensburg and Yakima, or from Yakima and Ellensburg to Seattle, carrying hiking boots in the truck or having left them in a closet at home, and to hear the abacadabra word, "Greenway," is instantly to receive the vision full and clear. Note the qualifier, "hiking boots." Other folks may be brought to see the light only by vigorous sermonizing. Not the wildland pedestrian. The trails preach eloquently and sufficiently. However, the hiker must take care never, in the throes of passion, to succumb to tunnel-vision anthropocentrism. Exercising the human bones, filling the human eyes, inspiring the human spirit, and playing with human toys are not the whole of "greenway"—nor even the most important to the human long run.

The Spokane writer known to us only as "Easy" has written, in a piece titled "Nature Corridors: A Global Link of Life,"

> Three hundred years ago, it is said, a squirrel could cross from the Mississippi to the Atlantic Ocean on the tree canopy without ever touching the ground. Today the squirrel could find superhighways to zip along and only a small number of disconnected nature corridors.... The nature corridors which remain today can be knit together to form continuous links across our globe. Our great nature areas including parks, forests, wilderness, and wetlands can be linked together.... National, state / provincial, county, and city nature areas can be interconnected.... It can be perfectly normal to expect to see areas of nature near our neighborhoods."

In 1990 a 5-day, 88-mile Mountains to Sound March was led by the Issaquah Alps Trails Club and Snoqualmie Valley Trails Club, departing from Snoqualmie Pass July 4 and arriving July 8 at Seattle's Waterfront Park. The press release for the event spoke to the question, "What is the proposed Mountains to Sound Trail?"

> It is not a single trail but a group of routes in a trail corridor. A continuous route (at least one) is envisioned that will permit pedestrian travel from Puget Sound to Snoqualmie Pass; most of the way east of Lake Washington will be motor-free, quiet. There will be a largely separate (but equal) continuous

route (at least one) for bicycle travel. From Issaquah east, there will be a continuous route (at least one) for horses.

On some stretches there will be multi-use routes accommodating pedestrians / horses or even pedestrians / horses / bicycles. However, uses will be mingled only where they are compatible.

Motorized travel will be prominent in the Greenway—scenic viewpoints, spots for family picnics and river play, and overnight camps for low-impact tenters. An excellent possibil-

Snoqualmie River Trail crossing a slough; Mount Si in distance

*ity exists for a low-speed (20 mph or less) scenic road system
from North Bend to Snoqualmie Pass. The road route already
is in place on the ground and needs only connections and recognition.*

*In conclusion, the Greenway trail corridor will have room
for every sort of recreational travel compatible with protection
of the land, the water, the plants, the wildlife—and compatible
with the nature-centered, non-kinetic, peace-and-quiet Greenway experience machine-burdened urbanites are crying for.*

*Last as well as first, the Greenway will serve as a "habitat
network" (the preferred new term for wildlife travel corridor)
connecting wilderness of the Cascades to wild nooks within the
urbanized core of Puget Sound City. In the phrase of Robinson
Jeffers, a human society must be "not man apart."*

In the fall of 1991, a non-profit consortium of environmentalists,
civic leaders, businesses, and governmental units from local to state
was incorporated—the Mountains to Sound Greenway Trust—with
James R. Ellis as president. The Trust for Public Land volunteered its
organizational skills and prepared an information leaflet:

*From Snoqualmie Pass to Puget Sound, our state high-
ways traverse a mosaic of green space. Family farms, state
parks, private timberland, national forests, and small towns
mark this journey from east to west. Today, much of this journey is green and scenic. We want to keep it that way for tomorrow, too. Growing communities need green space around them.
Working forests and farms depend on this land, and urban
dwellers need a refuge from the noise and pace of city life ... for
fishing and hiking ... for picnicking ... for the sheer pleasure of
a Sunday afternoon drive. If we take the green spaces we already have—public and private—and join them together to
create a Mountains to Sound Greenway, we can meet many of
our needs for open space. Today's vision can become tomorrow's
legacy.*

One last homily from the brochure:

*The saving of the green spirit of Puget Sound City would
be a model for elsewhere ... a refuge within, a place to breathe
deep and clean, to feel and think green peace, to recreate. A city
operates at high pressure in close quarters—it's the hot steam
of the boiler room that blasts out the great ideas that are civilization. However, too much heat boils the brains. Only by providing getaway space for a quick and easy cooling off can a city
keep on cooking.*

This was the vision of 1991. By 1993 it had burst bounds, tentatively spilling west over Puget Sound to Bremerton, definitely east beyond the Cascade Crest. Where to stop? The Kittitas Valley? No. The Yakima Valley? Perhaps. Independence, Missouri?

The vision of 1991 was not engendered from empty air. In 1981 a Mountains to Sound March was staged by The Mountaineers to dramatize the connection between the Alpine Lakes Wilderness and Seattle. In 1977 *Footsore 2,* predecessor of the present volume and now out of print (but check the library for a copy), suggested a "Cascade Gateway Recreation Area." In 1975 Stan Unger walked from Seattle to Snoqualmie Pass to publicize a proposed Sound to Mountains Trail. In the 1930s the "string of pearls" was bruited about the public press. In the 1920s Puget Sounders were enthralled by the call of the Yellowstone Highway. The Alaska-Yukon-Pacific Exposition featured the Guggenheim Trophy Race from New York to Seattle, crossing the Cascades via the pioneer-built wagon road. Nor was "greenway" a local invention. See the literature. A library of it.

A special sense about the Greenway here is that it could set off a regional epidemic. *Footsore 3* and *Footsore 4* note possibilities, such as the following:

- Whatcom County: Interurban Greenway south toward Mount Vernon; Bellingham Bay–Nooksack River–North Cascades National Park Greenway
- Skagit County: Anacortes–Skagit River–North Cascades National Park Greenway
- Snohomish County: Port Susan/Skagit Bay–North Fork Stillaguamish River–Glacier Peak Wilderness Greenway; South Fork Stillaguamish River–Mount Pilchuck–Monte Cristo Railroad–Henry M. Jackson Wilderness Greenway; Possession Sound–Snohomish Estuary–Skykomish River–Stevens Pass Greenway, to be extended as the Stevens Pass–Tumwater Canyon–Wenatchee–Columbia River Greenway
- Pierce County: Commencement Bay–Puyallup River–Foothills Trail–Carbon River–Mount Rainier National Park Greenway
- Thurston County: Nisqually National Wildlife Refuge–Nisqually River–Mount Rainier National Park Greenway

Eat one peanut and you can't stop until you finish the bag.

The History Feast

A publishing mini-industry flourishes on the subject of the Greenway. The westernmost stretch lies in *Footsore 1: Walks and*

Hikes around Puget Sound, flagship of the four-volume series in which this surveyor examined "the wildness within" and put before the citizenry the needs for its defense. The present book replaces (mostly) the out-of-print *Footsore 2.* Where the "wildness within" meets the "wildness without" of the National Wilderness Preservation System, it to a small extent overlaps *100 Hikes in Washington's Alpine Lakes* and *100 Hikes in Washington's South Cascades and Olympics,* two volumes of the "Hikes Series" dating from the 1960s. East of their areas, *55 Hikes in Central Washington* treats hiking in the steppe from Cascade forests to Wenatchee–Ellensburg–Yakima.

These all are Mountaineers books. So, too, is the 1981 classic (now out of print) *Snoqualmie Pass: From Indian Trail to Interstate,* by Yvonne Prater, who as a lifelong resident of Kittitas Valley ranchland knows the subject like her backyard, which it is. The temptation to ramble on about history has been stifled in favor of stipulating that every traveler of the Greenway must carry Yvonne's book in hand.

For several indispensable publications the student probably must go to a library. Mt. Baker–Snoqualmie National Forest has issued *Windows on the Past: Interpretive Guide to Pacific Northwest History* (1989); *A Cultural Resource Overview: Prehistory, Ethnography, and History* (1987); and *Snoqualmie Pass Wagon Road.*

A Greenway traveler can dream away hours at libraries in the course of old-timey Sunday Drives. The Association of King County Historical Organizations numbers seventy-odd member groups. Those that currently have Greenway-relevant museums are Black Diamond Historical Society, Bothell Historical Museum Society, Issaquah Historical Society, Maple Valley Historical Society, Marymoor Museum, Newcastle Historical Society, Puget Sound Railway Historical Museum, Renton Historical Society, and Snoqualmie Valley Historical Society.

The Issaquah Alps Trails Club, where the Greenway concept surfaced (after submarine bubbling) in the 1990s, has three books essential for the hiker/history buff: *Guide to Trails of Tiger Mountain State Forest,* by the Chief Ranger of the Issaquah Alps, William K. Longwell, Jr.; *Hiking and Strolling Trails of Cougar Mountain Regional Wildland Park,* by Harvey Manning and Ralph Owen; and *Coals of Newcastle,* by the late great historian Lucille MacDonald and son Richard.

In 1992 Tartu Publications did something completely different. Paul Dorpat, famed for his "Then and Now" photo comparisons in three books and the *Seattle Times,* produced *Seattle Chronicle,* a 2-hour VHS tape, a "collection of little stories strung end to end in order of time." See the beginnings of the Greenway in the heyday of that good old "Seattle Spirit" which made so much money for so few.

In the fall of 1993, Sasquatch Books published an absorbing history of the Greenway concept, *Mountains to Sound: The Creation of a Greenway across the Cascades,* a photograph-rich coffee-table book by Dan Chasan.

On the Greenway

In the words of a not-very-old folk song (pluck your guitar, a friend on harmonica), "When America finally goes to Hell, it's sure to figure how to get there sittin' down."

Millions of cars and trucks will continue to speed along "The Main Street of the Northwest" at or above 65 mph, a pace that satisfies an evident social and economic demand. It does not and cannot provide

Snoqualmie River Trail over Tolt River

what the federal Outdoor Recreation Review Commission hailed in the early 1960s as "America's favorite outdoor recreation, pleasure driving."

Those commissioners weren't looking at the world around them. They were remembering. So are we. We look to a revival of that olden-day pleasure driving, the Sunday-afternoon family tour that began when the tin lizzie and the merry Oldsmobile gave Americans "the freedom of the wheels," permitting folk of ordinary means to sortie from cities into the countryside. We have in mind a route in the mode of the old Sunset Highway. The upper speed limit might be set at the maximum of a family-loaded 1930 Model A Ford on the upgrade to Snoqualmie Falls; at 15 mph a person can both steer a car and watch jaybirds jump around in roadside trees; halts to let the radiator cool allow noses to investigate flowers. Honking the horn at a vehicle stopped in the middle of the road would be inexcusable; when a deer begs for a cookie, everyone must leap out of all the cars and come a-running with the Kodaks. Reader-boards at turnouts would tell the stories of the glaciers, the forests, the pioneers from Asia, and the late-comers from Europe. Picnic tables. Portable toilets (no sewers!). Self-guiding nature trails through woods to viewpoints, to the river for tossing pebbles and floating sticks. Tourism gridlock and excessive fuel consumption would be prevented by tour buses staged from North Bend and Seattle, from Cle Elum and Ellensburg.

Routes might be signed on logging roads no longer used for that purpose (no more trees) to provide the 4 x 4 adventurer and motorcy-clist (street-legal, highway-licensed driver) room for rough excitement. Dirtbike kinetics might be accommodated at designated spots on the Weyerhaeuser lands north of the Greenway.

The hiking community, which generated the concept, always has envisioned the Greenway as serving all users—that is, all the users the land can withstand. Motorless wheels would receive justice; the "skinny-tire" bicycle still lacks a pleasurable and safe route continuous from Puget Sound to Snoqualmie Pass and on east.

The "fat-tire" bicycle, newest of the "sittin' down" sports on the scene, lacks routes it can call its own and therefore is seeking space on existing foot trails. This cannot be done. Speeds of 2 mph and 10 mph, much less 20 mph, do not coexist. (Hikers are not selfishly excluding bikers from foot trails. The bikers are welcome. But not their bicycles.) Except where two conditions exist—(1) light traffic and (2) a very wide and long-sightlines route—the "multi-use trail" is a myth. (The Estab-lishment of playground-oriented parks departments and the multiple-use Forest Service wishes otherwise and, for the sake of getting home to dinner on time, strews the designation liberally about on maps. The Establishment encourages 2-mph and 20-mph travelers to put on happy faces and "share"; one supposes that at home the Establishment resolves disputes among neighborhood cats by dumping them all in a gunnysack and counseling them to purr.)

Spokespersons for the fat tires tend to have an orientation problem. Most have little if any knowledge of trail country and the wilderness concept; their travel mode did not achieve fad popularity until the late 1980s. Further, because the skinny-tire bicycle has been waging a righteous war for equality with the motorcar on the public highways, the rider transferring to the fat tires brings along the crusader's sense of sanctimony; additionally, because the sport is "muscle-powered" (in reality, it is as often gravity-powered), the rider supposes himself/herself the natural friend of the hikers who have devoted decades to building foot trails and assumes instant co-heirship to those decades of effort. The rider tends to be mortified, then angry, when his/her happy face is not answered by the like on hikers' faces. He/she has much to learn, starting with the manifest fact that the swift always will drive out the slow and that, polite or not, wheels expel feet, and that is not sharing, it is conquering. The Establishment places great faith in "education," surely necessary, but were it the full answer to social problems there would be no need for the police and penitentiaries. Before the fat tires can expect adult rights, they must accept adult responsibilities, must work to obtain routes by constructive efforts and rational discussion rather than tantrums.

A final category of wheels: At selected locations of opportunity there must be routes for the handicapped, including barrier-free paths for wheelchairs and self-guiding nature trails for the sightless, utilizing guide cords and Braille reader-boards.

A note on terminology: If a route is traveled by motor vehicles, it is a *road*. If it is traveled by non-motorized wheels, it is a *bikeway*. Only if travel is limited to feet is it a *trail*. "Jeep trail" and "motor nature trail" and "motorcycle trail" and "bicycle trail" are oxymorons. The term "trail" is habitually misapplied by public officials who hope that by this trick they can convince all the cats they are truly happy in the gunnysack. Granted, after a time all the cats still alive in the bag *will* be happy.

Of the sittin' down travel modes, the horse has the longest historical legitimacy. However, the size of the steeds and the dwindling of open space have pushed them steadily eastward until now, except for enclaves such as the Issaquah Alps, few bridle trails remain in Puget Sound City. Human-foot trails can serve hooves when traffic is light

Mount Si from Three Forks Regional Wildlife Park / Refuge

and the tread hard; abandoned rail grades and utility corridors surely can permit horse travel on a continuous line from the Issaquah Alps (possibly, with an effort, Lake Washington) to Snoqualmie Pass and the steppe. The expense of hardening trails for horses is so great that urban–suburban routes will be slow in coming and fast in disappearing. That's why many horsefolk are transferring their recreation—and their homes—to the "land lots of land under sunny skies above (don't fence me in)" east of the Cascades.

In summation, the travel mode that birthed the Greenway idea—walking—will and must continue to dominate the Greenway (except for I-90 itself, of course). This is the result partly of construction projects of volunteer hikers and very largely of the trail guides written by and for hikers; the fact that virtually all off-road traffic has been and still is on foot; the fact that walking is the poor person's sport, requiring no costly toys; the fact that walkers, being slow of pace, take up less room in the space–time continuum and, thus, fit better in a crowded world; and the fact that building routes for feet is comparatively cheap and easy—the "boot-built trail" is ubiquitous. Horse use and bicycle use entail large expenditures. Because this use is by small minorities, they must recognize that the limited amounts of public funds require them to supplement their proper share of these funds by private contributions and volunteer construction. Attempts to employ the strategy of conquest would only delay full justice.

On Foot

Foot travel includes "walks," short excursions on easy paths in forgiving terrain, requiring no special clothing or equipment and no experience or training, and "hikes," longer and/or rougher, potentially dangerous, demanding stout shoes or boots, clothing for cold and wet weather, gear for routefinding and emergencies, rucksack to carry it all in, and best done in the company of experienced companions or eased into gradually.

Herein are described short walks suitable for a leisurely afternoon or even a spring-summer evening as well as long walks that may keep a person hopping all day. For any walk, equipment demands no more than a passing thought; as for technique, the rule is just to pick 'em up and lay 'em down and look both ways before crossing the street.

Hikes are another matter, and the novice must take care when choosing a trip to be aware of the difference and to make appropriate preparations. The novice should review a general hiking manual, such as *Backpacking: One Step at a Time* (New York: Vintage Books, 1986). On every hike where a shout for help might not bring quick assistance to the lost or injured or ill, each person should carry the Ten Essentials:

1. Extra clothing—enough so that if a sunny-warm morning yields to a rainy-windy afternoon, or if an accident keeps the party out overnight, hypothermia ("exposure" or "freezing to death") will not be a threat.
2. Extra food—enough so something is left over at the planned end of the trip, in case the actual end is the next day.
3. Sunglasses—if travel on snow for more than a few minutes may be involved.
4. Knife—for first aid and emergency firebuilding (making kindling).
5. Firestarter—a candle or chemical fuel for starting a fire with wet wood.
6. First aid kit.
7. Matches—in a waterproof container.
8. Flashlight—with extra bulb and batteries.
9. Map.
10. Compass.

Information summaries for trips generally contain the following information.

"Round trip xx miles" and "elevation gain $xxxx$ feet" tell a person if the trip fits his/her energy and ambition.

"Allow x hours" must be used with a personal conversion factor. The figures here are based on doing about 1½ miles an hour on the flat (walking at a pace of 2 miles an hour but walking only 45 minutes in the hour) and an elevation gain of about 700 feet an hour.

"High point $xxxx$ feet" tells much about the vegetation and views to expect, but especially the probable amount of snow in any given month.

"All year" or "February–December" or whatever rudely spells this out. The intent is to tell when, in an average normal year (whatever that is), a trail is probably sufficiently snowfree for pleasure walking, meaning less than a foot of snow or only occasional deeper patches. Several factors are involved. One is elevation. Another is distance from Puget Sound, whose large volume of above-freezing water warms winter air masses. In any locality, higher is generally snowier. But also, for identical elevations the farther from saltwater is generally snowier. And mountain valleys, acting like giant iceboxes, generally are snowier than nearby lowlands outside the mountain front. Finally, though south and west slopes get as much snow as north and east ones, they also get more sun (and also more sun than valley flats) and thus melt out faster.

Maps to Tie the Land Together

The aim of our guidebooks is to teach a person how to tie the land together with his/her feet and eyes. Maps are valuable aids.

For each section the contour maps are noted. The U.S. Geological Survey (USGS) maps are the basics. Better for the hiker, where available, are the Green Trails maps; the private publisher puts green overprints on USGS base maps to show current roads and trails, the data updated every other year.

Robert Kinzebach publishes *Pic-Tour Guide Maps,* aerial photos and USGS sheets with the findings of his personal explorations overprinted.

For broad orientation, pictorial landform maps are superb. *Puget Sound Region, Washington,* by Dee Molenaar, was designed and produced specifically at the request of this surveyor to cover the area from the Olympics to the Cascades, Canada to Chehalis, permitting the hiker to be related at all times to all horizons. Particularly helpful is a condensed textbook in the margin, a history of the geologic structures and the Pleistocene glaciers; the pictorial map of the maximum extent of the Puget Lobe of the Cordilleran Ice Sheet explains innumerable terrain features that baffle the uninformed eye.

Richard Pargeter has two similar maps of somewhat different coverage. *The Puget Sound Country: A View from the Northwest* and *Washington's Northwest Passage: A View from the Southwest* cover most of the *Footsore* country and the Greenway as well.

These and others are sold at hiking shops and map specialty stores.

Camping

The Greenway has two sorts of backcountry: Alpine Lakes Wilderness and everything else.

Fragile ecosystems of the Wilderness are so overstressed that Mt. Baker–Snoqualmie National Forest is conducting continuing studies to determine where the land can accept camping, by how many campers, and in what manner. The subject is discussed in *100 Hikes in Washington's Alpine Lakes.* Our personal feeling is that the Greenway section of the Alpine Lakes Wilderness ought to be primarily day-use only.

Yet to be studied is the potential for trail camping in the non-Wilderness section of the Greenway. It must not be forgotten that some of this land has been proposed for addition to the Wilderness and in the

North Fork Gorge

interim must be managed as if it already were in the Wilderness. As for the other, we would not presume to spell out at this time the proper management of the Mount Si Natural Resources Conservation Area, the Mount Si Highline, the North Ridge, the South Ridge, and Rattlesnake Mountain. We hope that campsites can be developed on these hiking trails, hardened to withstand human impact, and supplied with such sanitation facilities as may be indicated. Canny wildlanders know now the great spots to spread a bag and watch the nova of megalopolis complete with stars overhead.

One sure thing about all the backcountry, in Wilderness and out, is that wood fires are or will be banned just about everyplace. Carry a backpacker stove and an extra sweater.

Litter and Garbage and Sanitation

If you can carry it in full, you can carry it out empty. Take back to the car every can, foilwrap, and orange peel.

Never bury garbage. If fresh, animals will dig it up and scatter the remnants. Burning before burying is no answer either. Tin cans take as long as 40 years to disintegrate completely; aluminum and glass last for centuries. Further, digging pits to bury junk disturbs the ground cover, and iron eventually leaches from buried cans and "rusts" springs and creeks.

Keep the water pure. Don't wash dishes in streams or lakes, loosing food particles and detergent. Haul buckets of water off to the woods or rocks and wash and rinse there.

Eliminate body wastes in places well removed from watercourses; first dig a shallow hole in the "biological disposer layer," then touch a match to the toilet paper (but not in forest-fire season!)—better, use leaves—and finally cover the evidence. So managed, the wastes are consumed in a matter of days. Where privies are provided, use them. On more and more trails, the rule is to carry a double bag and transport your solid wastes out of the wildlands.

Water

A word to the wise: For Greenway hiking, fill your canteens at home and give the matter no further thought.

In the late 1970s began a great epidemic of giardiasis, caused by a vicious little parasite that spends part of its life cycle swimming free in water and part in the intestinal tract of beavers and other wildlife, dogs, and people. Actually, the "epidemic" was solely in the press; *Giardia* were first identified in the eighteenth century and are present in the public water systems of many cities of the world and many towns in America—including some in the foothills of the Cascades. Long before the "outbreak" of "beaver fever," there was the well-known malady the "Boy Scout trots," which in the era of foreign travel became the "Aztec two-step" and "the revenge of the Pharaohs." This is not to make light of the disease: though most humans feel no ill effects (but become carriers), others have symptoms that include devastating diarrhea; the treatment is nearly as unpleasant. The reason giardiasis has become "epidemic" is that there are more people in the backcountry—more people drinking water contaminated by animals—more people contaminating the water.

Melakwa Lake

Whenever in doubt, boil the water 10 minutes. Keep in mind that *Giardia* can survive in water at or near freezing for weeks or months—a snow pond is not necessarily safe. Boiling is 100 percent effective against not only *Giardia* but the myriad other filthy little blighters that may upset your digestion or—as with some forms of hepatitis—destroy your liver. *If you cannot boil,* use one of the several iodine treatments (chlorine compounds have been found untrustworthy in wildland circumstances), such as Potable Aqua or the more complicated method that employs iodine crystals. Rumor to the contrary, iodine treatments pose no threat to the health. *Be very wary* of the filters sold in backpacking shops: don't bet your liver on a manufacturer's "guarantees."

Theft

Equipment has become so fancy and expensive, and hikers so numerous, that theft is a growing trailhead industry. Not even backcountry camps are entirely safe, but the professionals concentrate on cars. Rangers have the following recommendations.

Don't make crime profitable. If the pros break into a hundred cars and get nothing but moldy boots and tattered T shirts they'll go straight. The best bet is to arrive in a beat-up 1960 car with doors and windows that don't close and leave in it nothing of value. If you insist on driving a nice new car, at least don't have mag wheels, tape deck, and radio, and keep it empty of gear. Don't think locks help—pros can open your car door and trunk as fast with a picklock as you can with your key. Don't imagine you can hide anything from them—they know all the hiding spots.

Be suspicious of anyone waiting at a trailhead. One of the tricks of the trade is to sit there with a pack as if waiting for a ride, watching new arrivals unpack—and hide their valuables—and maybe even striking up a conversation to determine how long the marks will be away.

The ultimate solution, of course, is for hikers to become as poor as they were in the olden days. No criminal would consider trailheads profitable if the loot consisted solely of shabby khaki war surplus.

A Note About Safety

Safety is an important concern in all outdoor activities. No guide-book can alert you to every hazard or anticipate the limitations of every reader. Therefore, the descriptions of roads, trails, routes, and natural features in this book are not representations that a particular place or excursion will be safe for your party. When you follow any of the routes described in this book, you assume responsibility for your own safety. Under normal conditions, such excursions require the usual attention to traffic, road and trail conditions, weather, terrain, the capabilities of your party, and other factors. Keeping informed on current conditions and exercising common sense are the keys to a safe, enjoyable outing.

The Mountaineers

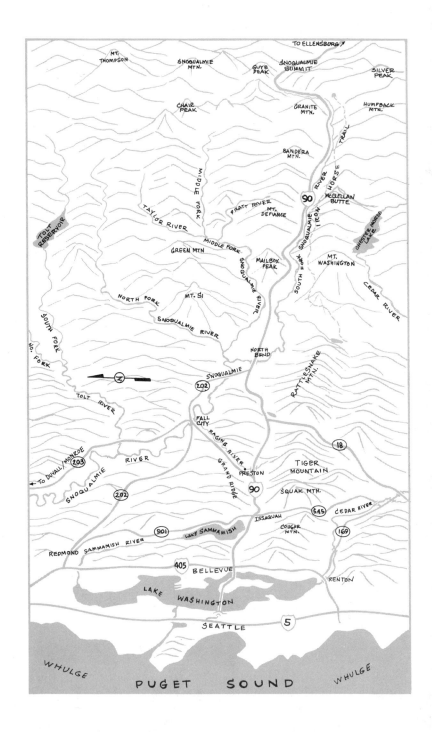

East from the Whulge to the Issaquah Alps

In Lushootseed, the language spoken from the Skagit River to southern reaches of the estuary, it was *Whulge,* translated as "the saltwater" or "the saltwater we know." European-Americans couldn't get their tongues around that, chose a new name, and set about building "Puget Sound City." There, in Seattle, on Elliott Bay, the Greenway starts.

Being a walker's guide, the present book leaves to others the values and functions of the Greenway. It further leaves to a companion volume, *Footsore 1,* the walking in Seattle and immediately east. However, to completely portray pedestrianism from the Whulge to the Cascade Crest, we here outline footpaths from tidewater to the Issaquah Alps.

The walker ought not start east at all until he/she has firm footing on the west. Workaday has moved mostly north and south, leaving the old work waterfront, Alaskan Way (nee Railroad Avenue), mainly a play waterfront, with shops and restaurants and museums and parks. But it also is the History Waterfront. Yesler's mill. The coals of Newcastle. The Great Fire. The gold of the Yukon. The silk of Japan. The fish of the Whulge and the Gulf of Alaska. The mosquito fleet which steamed the Water Road from milltowns to their cultural center, the Skid Road. Pioneer Place, as the walker now knows it. Gold Rush National Historic Park. Terminus of the long-gone Seattle-Tacoma Interurban Railway.

Feet ascend east up the (long-gone) cablecar route to the summit of First Hill, then Second Hill, and descend to Lake Washington. In 1987 the mayor of Seattle, Charles Royer, declared, "Our open spaces—our parks and boulevards—form our image of the city. If we are to keep Seattle the most livable city, a place in which to raise our children, we need to preserve, not just our individual neighborhoods, but the open spaces throughout the city that we all cherish." At the lake the walkway passes through Frink and Leschi Parks, segments of the city-traversing "Olmstead Legacy." Writ large, it embodies the vision of the Greenway.

From the Leschi ferry dock (long gone), the feet turn south to the Mercer Island Floating Bridge, whose sidewalks enable non-motorized

Snoqualmie flood plain from the Snoqualmie River Trail near Griffin Creek; Tiger Mountain in background

crossing of the "Big Water." Mercer Island has a bikeway utilizing a lid park atop I-90. The pedestrian turns left on little old Mercer Way through old neighborhoods to Luther Burbank (King County) Park on the lakeshore.

Matters improve on the mainland. On the north side of the Greenway, Bellevue City Parks begins its offerings with Mercer Slough Nature Park, which connects to Bellevue Community College Greenbelt, Bellefields Nature Park, Kelsey Creek Park, Wilburton Hill Park, Robinswood Park, Lake Hills Greenbelt, and Weowna Park on the breaks to Lake Sammamish. Though the city has only the skinniest of alleyways to the Big Water and the "Little Water" (Lake Sammamish), between the two it has preserved the most an6d the best wetlands (bog, marsh, swamp) park system in King County, sensitively sampled by its Lake-to-Lake Parkway Trail.

On the south side of I-90, Bellevue's Newcastle Beach Park is a beauty bit on the delta of Coal Creek (the entire delta would have become park had King County not been twiddling thumbs). In sequence east are Coal Creek (King County) Park and, not far to the south, May Creek (King County) Park, crucial elements in the habitat network/ trail entryway to Cougar Mountain Regional Wildland Park, King County's largest park and the largest in-urban wildland park in the nation.

I-90 climbs between these greens to a divide at Eastgate and descends to the Issaquah Plain and Lake Sammamish. On the way it passes beneath the Cougar Mountain Precipice, a virgin forest magically preserved close above the freeway, harboring a zoo of wildlife

Reinig Bridge and Mount Si

from bear to cougar and coyote down in size to the aplodontia and shrew.

Sprawling over the Issaquah Plain is "The Trailhead City." North of the freeway is Lake Sammamish State Park, the most heavily used in the state system; a trail is proposed along the lake to hitch to the Sammamish River Trail, which hitches to the Burke-Gilman Trail/ Bikeway and the Tolt Pipeline Trail, which combine to hitch Puget Sound City to the Cascades. South of the freeway is Squak Mountain State Park, a natural area so strictly preserved under terms of the donor, the Bullitt family, that no technology more advanced than boots is permitted.

At the east edge of Issaquah, the freeway dives into the sinuous green canyon of East Fork Issaquah Creek, birthplace of the Greenway idea and quintessence of what it's all about. The idea's supreme triumph to date has been Tiger Mountain State Forest, "a working forest in an urban environment." The large portion immediately above the freeway does other work than producing wood fiber, having been set aside by the state legislature as the West Tiger Mountain Natural Resources Conservation Area, the closest approach in state land management to a National Wilderness as defined by Congress in 1964.

Tiger forms the south wall of the green canyon. The breaks on the north rise steeply to Grand Ridge, scene of as bitter a battle as local history has witnessed between the Greens and the Grays. Not entirely outside the battle lines is the historic village of Preston.

Preston lies on the Raging River, Seattle's closest "mountain river." It is, as well, *the* river of the Issaquah Alps, flowing from Tiger, Taylor, and Rattlesnake, cleaving Tiger from Rattlesnake and Grand Ridge from Snoqualmie Ridge, aka Lake Alice Plateau. Though the Issaquah Alps include Rattlesnake, the Raging River is a natural boundary between here and there. *Footsore 1* quits at the Raging; out-of-print *Footsore 2* picked up there. This new book carries on eastward into the future.

Snoqualmie Valley:
Upstream to the North Bend Plain

USGS maps: Carnation, Fall City, Lake Joy, Snoqualmie, North Bend,
*   Bandera*
Green Trails map: Bandera

West of Snoqualmie Valley rise Grand Ridge-Mitchell Hill and the East Sammamish Plateau, where debate rages over how many New Cities to build and where and how much open space to leave green and quiet to cleanse the air, refresh the human spirit, and let wildlife roam.

East and north of Snoqualmie Valley, in the angle where the river sharply changes direction, lies the Great Big Western Tree Farm. Clearcut by railroad loggers and again by truck loggers, the expectation has been that it would remain a permanent base for the forest industry of centuries to come, the topography and elevation ideal for growing trees to harvest size in 40 years. This GBWTF would simultaneously provide varied logging-road recreations, some of its routes open to motors, others reserved for silent wheels, and others for human and equine feet. Last but not least, it would constitute the permanent boundary of Puget Sound City, forever safe from urbanization, suburbanization, and exurbanization. Will this happen? Most of the land is private. Protecting the public interest from the bottom line of free enterprise will require public actions.

As the century moved into its second half, Snoqualmie Valley itself seemed doomed to be housed and officed and shopping-centered and blacktopped with no debate whatsoever. However, the State Wildlife Department struck a blow for the Greens by acquiring some 1500 acres (2½ square miles) of riverbank and floodplain, a Snoqualmie Habitat Management Area where hunters and fisherfolk take their pleasure in the company of birders, flowerers, and plain and simple pedestrians. Not to forget the wildlife.

King County then struck three mighty blows. First, it adopted a policy of snapping up rights-of-way as fast as railroads abandoned them, before privatizers could clutch them, thereby enabling foot trails/horse trails/bikeways from city's edge to mountain front. Second, in 1979 under King County Executive John Spellman, voters approved

Farms along the Snoqualmie River Trail north of Duvall

a Farmlands Preservation Program, to buy development rights from farmers so they could continue farming free from prohibitive taxes made inevitable by the steamroller of developers and free, too, of the temptation to sell out to developers. During the 1980s, under King County Executive Randy Revelle, some 5000 acres, more than 7 square miles, were thus preserved of the flat green floodplain meandered by the river, embellished with cutoff sloughs, oxbow lakes, and marshes, decorated by picturesque barns and heaps of manure. Third, in 1992 the King County Council adopted a Sensitive Areas Ordinance, an implicit expression of the Public Trust Doctrine, a 1500-year-old tenet of the common law that requires the government to protect the public interest in lands, privately owned or not, of public importance. Sensitive wetlands, for example.

Over and above all this, Nature Conservancy has acquired and set aside a Snoqualmie Bog Preserve and the Audubon Society a Carnation Marsh Sanctuary, each some 100 acres in 1994 and growing as funds are contributed.

Good starts. Not enough, of course. More preserves and sanctuaries are a primary urgency. Most of the farmlands still are outside the county program, "held for development." Yet surely when the Great Spirit looks down upon the *Sdoh-kwahl-bu,* as the Original Residents called the river, He/She says, "Lo! It is good, very good. Well, *pretty good.*"

There are peaceful nooks to watch water ripple and fish swim, ducks paddle and dippers dip and herons flap, to scuff along a gravel bar and skip stones. In season there are berries and peas and corn and garlic to buy from farmers, such fresh food as few Puget Sounders have known since local sources of produce were replaced by the Imperial Valley and Mexico. Children can be introduced to a cow and informed, "That's who fills up the milk cartons."

The trails are close to city homes and at elevations open to walking the year around, rarely cluttered by deep snow and only now and then by deep water.

Snoqualmie River Trail
(Maps—pages 36, 41)

One way from Duvall to Cedar Falls junction 35 miles
High point 1029 feet, elevation gain about 1000 feet
All year
Bus: Metro 210 (on Highway 202)

Walk from near-tidewater dairy farms to mountain-front tree farms. See the water flow and the corn grow, the trees rise up and up, then fall down and down, temporarily opening big views. Bring a pad to sketch the barns, binoculars to spy on otters and dickybirds. Ponder the evolution of transportation technology: the rail bridges of the Chicago, Milwaukee, St. Paul, and Pacific, constructed when folks were still hale and hearty who had been on hand to marvel when America built its first railroads; the Model T bridges of the 1920s Sunset Highway, the V-8

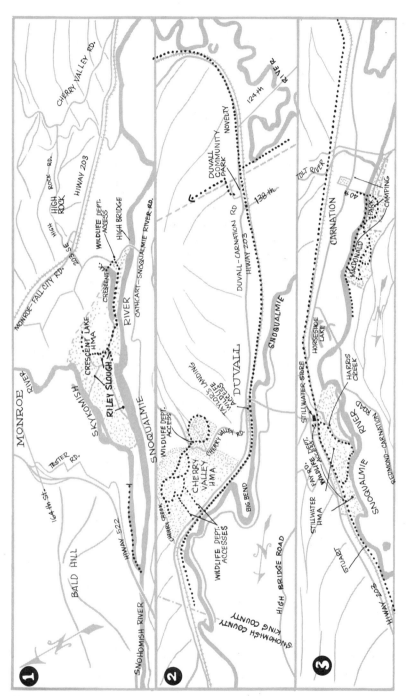

36

bridges of the 1940s U.S. 10, and the Armageddon bridges of the 1980s Interstate 90; and for poignant contrast, the bikeway/trail that has inherited the Milwaukee grade.

As of 1994 the trail is partly maintained and peaceful under King County Parks jurisdiction, partly languishing in neglect and lawless uproar under the same jurisdiction, and partly under no visible jurisdiction whatsoever.

The long-distance walkers who plod from sea to sea to improve their souls and destroy their soles and gain enduring (10 minutes) fame will wish to walk the complete route, probably very fast. Ordinary folks will take their pleasure in morning constitutionals and evening saunters and all-day tramps, starting from Highway 203, Highway 202, North Bend Way, Cedar Falls Way, and Cedar Falls Road.

Monroe to Duvall, 9½ miles

Skip it. Snohomish County was expected to acquire the 6 miles from Monroe south to the King County line. Didn't. The magnificent

Entrance to Taylor Landing Boat Launch at Duvall

Skykomish River bridge survives, but you can't get anywhere from there.

South of the King County line, the grade is beside the highway to Duvall, okay for joggers except where the hellberries and barbed wire and dogs are fierce.

Duvall to Stillwater, 6½ miles

When Duvall gets serious it will clean up the riverbank and talk up the history of Taylor's Landing, located at the north end of town and now the site of a State Wildlife parking lot.

South from the town's homely backside, the trail heads out in floodplain pastures. Watch for muskrats in murky swamps, blackbirds

Farm along Snoqualmie River Trail near Fay Road

in the cattails, and red-tailed hawks circling above on the lookout for stupid chickens.

At 1½ miles from town center (church, bookstore) is Duvall Community Park. The best access to the trail is the Tolt Pipeline service road, a bit south of the park.

The 1 mile south from the park to 124th (Novelty Hill Road) is in the quiet apart from the highway, in broad cross-valley views. Very nice. South of 124th the way is beside the highway 1¾ miles. Leave it to the dog-exercisers and joggers.

The next 1¼ miles, to Fay Road, are a delight. In ¼ mile is a slough crossed by a trestle with a dozen 16-foot spans between "bents." The excellent mile south of here is most esthetically walked from the south end at Fay Road. The grade quickly quits the highway racket and is bounded for nearly ½ mile by cattail marsh. It then emerges into pastures and where used to be the rail station of "Stuart" (so says the map) touches wild river—not channelized, not diked. Do the rotten palisades date from a landing for the steamers en route to the head of navigation (Fall City)? Views extend up and down meanders and over fields to far mountains. Beyond the green plain the eye is caught by the candy-cute pink-and-white buildings of Carnation Farms (tour visitors welcome). In a grove of impressive cottonwoods (no morels, the cows eat 'em up), the grade comes to the handsome trestle.

The last ¾ mile south from Fay Road to Stillwater lies in the Snoqualmie Habitat Management Area (see "Stillwater"), where the wild things are.

Stillwater to Griffin Creek Road (NE 11), 5 miles

Stillwater Store is one of the oldest surviving country stores in King County and probably the closest to Seattle. So stop in and buy something.

The 1¼ miles south from Stillwater are serene because while the highway hugs the valley wall the grade strikes off across the valley floor. Walk slowly to see the strawberries ripen; in early summer buy a box to eat afoot; in late summer buy fresh-picked corn, hurry home, and immerse the ears in rapidly boiling water no longer than 3 minutes. Be quick about it, because in 24 to 36 hours the sugar in the kernels turns to starch, and that's why store corn and farm corn are two different species.

The trail crosses the highway to a 3-mile due-south straightaway through Carnation. Beyond town the woods close in. The Tolt River bridge is a classic.

Griffin Creek Road (NE 11) to Spring Glen Road (356 SE), 6¾ miles

To here the trail has been on the floodplain below Snoqualmie Falls. Now it sets about sidehill-gouging upward to the floodplain above Snoqualmie Falls. Though hillside pastures let the big sky in, the mood is mainly woods, an alternation of big old conifers and maples, monoculture plantations of Douglas fir being farmed as if it were corn, and clearcuts that for a while will let in the hot sun and give wide views. Private driveways climbing from the valley to and across the rail line warn that Puget Sound City wants to advance onto the Tokul Plateau and eastward to the Cascade front and no doubt up the scarp as far as megabucks can afford.

Snoqualmie River Trail near Fay Road

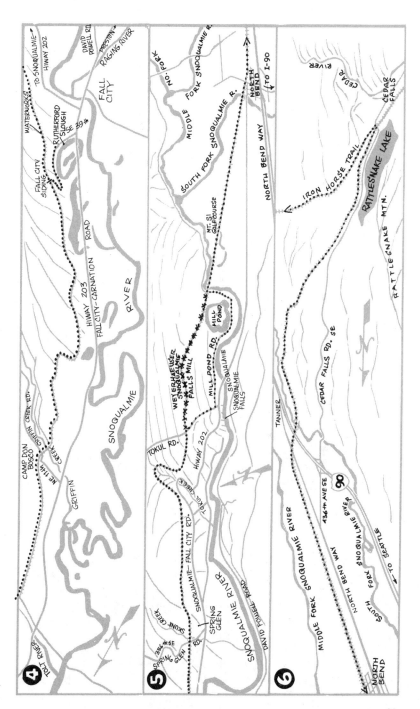

41

Beyond the Griffin Creek trestle and its esthetic twenty-five bents, the trail curves out to scenic promontories and into waterfall gulches, some spanned by bridges (between Cherry Creek and Tokul Creek there are, or used to be, thirty-three).

At 3½ miles is the site of Fall City Siding. To drive here, turn off Highway 203 on SE 39 Street, follow the curving shore of Rutherford Slough (a mile-long oxbow that excites the bird-haunted fancy), and attain the grade at 293 feet, 1.2 miles from the highway.

Here the river turns in its seaward course from westerly to northerly. The siding overlooks both segments of the valley with their mosaics of man's plane-table right-anglings (Greek-like) and Nature's hydraulic meanderings and twirlings (Arab-like). Beyond clusters of homes and ribbons of roads tower the Issaquah Alps.

In ½ mile from the siding is the abandoned Fall City Waterworks, tapping a fine big creek sliced deep in glacier droppings, crying out to be drunk but likely infested with *Giardia,* as what isn't nowadays. In another scant ½ mile, an eighteen-span trestle was pulled down to prevent a tragic collapse under the weight of a horse or the thudding of a jogger. Views from the west end of the trestle site are down to Snoqualmie River and Raging River, Fall City, golf course, and highway; across to proposed New Cities on Snoqualmie Ridge and Grand Ridge-Mitchell Hill; and to Rattlesnake and Tiger Mountains. A scant 2¼ miles more is Spring Glen Road.

Spring Glen Road (356 SE) to Tokul Road, 2½ miles

From Highway 202 Spring Glen Road ascends 0.2 mile to the trail, a handy start for walks in either direction.

The task of the railroad easterly from here was to climb from lower valley to upper with a less abrupt gradient than that of Snoqualmie Falls, whose brink is at 400 feet and plunge basin at 120. At 1½ miles is the scene of a more formidable challenge, the crossing of Tokul Creek gorge, the dramatic climax of the route. It would have been even more exciting had Europeans arrived a century or so later because by then Tokul Creek, which had been wont to carry the overflow of Snoqualmie floods, would have captured the entire river, probably on a dark and stormy night. A valley train of alluvium would have raised havoc all the way to Everett; Snoqualmie Falls would have been left high and dry except for seeps and drips, as is the case now when Puget Power is transmuting all the water into gold.

Views are excellent where the grade begins its swing through the canyon; the 1980s clearcut is a foreground for Mount Si and Tiger Mountain. The trestle, too, thrills the acrophobe, though it has been

Tokul Creek Bridge

planked and is perfectly safe, as it was not for the planker, who fell to his death. The grade swings ⅔ mile out of the canyon and in another ⅓ mile tunnels under Tokul Road. To drive here, go off Highway 202 at the east edge of Snoqualmie Falls Park on Tokul Road. Bear left at a Y and in 0.5 mile, just short of the tunnel, park on the shoulder, elevation 500 feet.

Tokul Road to Reinig Bridge, 2 miles

Three-quarters of the clockway to the century mark, Snoqualmie Falls Mill is a poor bet to finish the course. The sawmill, built in 1916 to slice up ancient trees, was torn down in 1989. Storage sheds and depopulated emptiness remain—and a stack that poops out photogenic billows of steam, nostalgic foreground for Rattlesnake Mountain.

But just now you can't really get there from anywhere, not afoot. Weyerhaeuser Company doesn't want folks walking the 2 miles of young (yawn) forests leading into and out of its parking lot. Until government can strike a deal, pay the asking price, or muster the courage to wield its rights of adverse possession and public trust, Snoqualmie River Trail will have to detour via Tokul Road, Mill Pond Road, and Reinig Road. In fact, the possibility exists that an irritated Weyerhaeuser might haul off and totally obliterate the grade in the vicinity of Tokul Creek, where King County apparently has failed to acquire a piece of company land.

Until the matter is settled, skip the 2 miles.

Reinig Bridge to North Bend, 2½ miles

From Railroad Avenue, the main drag of the town of Snoqualmie, turn north on Meadowbrook Avenue. Across the river Meadowbrook joins Mill Pond Road to become Reinig Road. At 0.3 mile from the junction is the Reinig rail bridge, "Built by the Pennsylvania Steel Co. Steelton Pa. 1910."

Pause on the bridge for a photo of the river and Mount Si. Proceed onto the second floodplain of the journey. A short path invites the picnic basket to a gravel bar. At a long ½ mile from the bridge, a farm lane leads ¼ mile to a larger bar. In a long ¾ mile from the bridge, the grade crosses Meadowbrook Slough to the entry road of Mt. Si Golf Course. To drive here, go north from Snoqualmie on Meadowbrook Avenue and turn right 0.7 mile on Park Street.

Semi-improved to a service road, the grade cuts through the golf course, whose civil greensward and sculptured firs and cherubic golfers are foreground for artistic photos of Mount Si and Rattlesnake.

Weyerhaeuser mill from near town of Snoqualmie

In 1¾ miles from the golf course entry, the way passes cows and woods, crosses birdy sloughs and the South Fork Snoqualmie, and comes out on Main Avenue at the west edge of beautiful downtown North Bend. Elevation, 440 feet.

All the flat land the eye sees in this floodplain walk was, in 1880, the largest hop farm in the world. Something on the order of a square mile remains undeveloped in Meadowbrook Farm and Tollgate Farm, described by the mayor of North Bend as "one of the last pieces of un-spoiled farm land ... part of our natural heritage that must be saved for our children and grandchildren."

What I-90 traveler witnessing the transformation of the Issaquah Plain in the past decade and much of the North Bend Plain in the past half-decade cannot agree? Many eyes are focused on these pastures, which in recent years have fed a few cows, exported a little silage, but mostly remained dormant awaiting their fate. King County Parks has committed to purchase 60 acres of the wettest wetlands for the Three Forks Regional Wildlife Park/Refuge. (In objective ecological estimation, virtually the entire farmland is wetland.) An opinion held by many minds is that the complete Meadowbrook tract should be purchased by the public or otherwise preserved by obtaining development rights or applying rationally rigid zoning and combined with Tollgate Farm and the Three Forks Park to create a super-park. A developer has a proposal to dedicate 400 acres as open space if given permission to dry up 60 acres for dense development. A proposal of greater appeal is to devote some of the open space to the flooding needs of the river and the floodwaters-retention role of the pastures and a substantial portion to a non-conflicting horticultural interpretive center where historic crops would be raised and harvested, to the awe and admiration of little children who cannot travel to California to see food in the field and suppose the carrots and peas and lettuce in supermarkets are manufactured by machines in the backrooms.

North Bend (Main Avenue) to Tanner, 3½ miles

Sojourners from afar find little here to light up their eyes. The grade can be traced through the city to Ballarat Avenue, where it is signed "15 mph," a brisk pace for a pedestrian. The way turns rural and woodsy, featuring cows and close views of Little Si. Two paved sideroads are crossed and then, at 3 miles, North Bend Way (old U.S. 10), identifiable by a blacktop patch cutting across the concrete. Here, at the edge of what the pioneers called Sallal Prairie, at the site of Tanner (best known nowadays for Tanner Rural Electrical Cooperative, a perennial populist thorn in the side of Puget Power, reminding of the era when Eastern monopolists sought to legally forbid public power), is the intersection of Tanner Road and North Bend Way. Here, too, is the eastern terminus of the Gilman Railroad (Northern Pacific, it became, then Burlington-Northern, then zip) from North Bend, Issaquah, Redmond, Seattle, Ballard. Terminus elevation, 520 feet.

Tanner to Cedar Falls, 6¾ miles

This is more like. The task of the railroad here was to ascend from the North Bend Plain to intersect the Milwaukee's mainline, which had been completed through Snoqualmie Pass in 1909. The deed was done by rounding the toe of "Boxley Mountain" (a semi-detached segment of the Canadian moraine) to the valley of Boxley Creek and following it up to the Seattle City Water community of Cedar Falls. Until recently the route could be walked without seeing hide nor hair of another human. But suburbanization is gridding up the forests and exurbanization is spawning a proliferation of hideaways. By the turn of the century, the solitary pedestrian might have to take a look around before scratching. But not quite yet.

Maybe not ever, if the public plays its cards right. The residents of those suburbs, exurbs, and hideaways have brushed out on their private property a system of hiker/horse paths connecting to the old rail grade. As trail-travelers themselves, they empathize with non-landed walkers/horses and point to a Greenway opportunity. Large tracts of property that abut the rail grade presently are for sale at reasonable prices. Large tracts owned by the state and the county seem to be unknown to the state and the county. A splendid stretch of always-green

Mailbox Peak from Snoqualmie River Trail near Cedar Falls

trail could link a series of passive parks where spacious forests would be permitted to grow old in peace, parks where walkers could pause for refreshment.

Walks can start at either end; the lower (northern) end is far the better. Midpoint accesses from Cedar Falls Road and near the end of Edgewick Road in the valley of Boxley Creek might be provided but are not presently open. Fill your eyes with the possibilities and go home and write a letter to somebody.

To start at Tanner, drive North Bend Way 1.7 miles east from its split from Cedar Falls Way, the other half of old U.S. 10. Park at Tanner Road. The grade sets out as a wide gravel road past the site of Tanner Mill, destined to become a vast parking lot for Puget Power service vehicles. In ¼ mile are the spray-painted underpinnings of I-90 and a steel railway bridge over the South Fork Snoqualmie. The next 1½ miles are beside or near the river and woodland homes of River Bend; traffic of walkers, joggers, and dog-exercisers is heavy. The grade reaches the frontier of suburbia, climbs onto the toe of 1040-foot Boxley Mountain, and sidehills around the corner into green-wild Boxley Creek valley.

At 3¼ miles from River Bend, the grade passes Rainbow "Lake." Driving past here on Cedar Falls Road, a narrow sideroad can be spotted to the rail grade. Park on the highway shoulder, elevation 880 feet.

The final 1¾ miles beside Cedar Falls Road take the grade through Rattlesnake Gap (route of the Really Big River, which once carried the waters of all the Cascade rivers emanating from the north on a southward quest for the Pacific Ocean), along Rattlesnake Lake, a sink of seepage through the moraines from the Cedar River, to the junction with the Milwaukee mainline from Maple Valley and Renton. The junction is exactly where Cedar Falls Road crosses both former rail grades. Junction elevation, 970 feet.

At the junction the mainline goes straight ahead into the Cedar River Watershed, closed to walkers, and straight behind on what eventually will be the start of Iron Horse Trail.

Note: As of this writing the final mile of the rail grade/trail is signed "No Trespassing" and means it. Seattle City Water is preparing a revised boundary-management plan that will open certain watershed-edge stretches to the public feet. Until the plan is perfected and implemented, obey the signs. Do not walk the grade all the way to the Cedar Falls junction. Use the Rainbow Lake access. (To be straight with the reader, the start at Tanner is the only one appealing to other than local folks.)

Snoqualmie Habitat Management Area
(Map—page 36)

The State Wildlife Department has bought easements on 9 miles of the Snoqualmie River, innumerable spots to feed fishes and bother birds. Except for gravel bars there is little walking. To be intimate with the river, float.

However, the feet have room to roam in the Snoqualmie Habitat Management Area (HMA), formerly called a Wildlife Recreation Area on the anthropocentric assumption that the most fun wildlife ever have is getting shot at and et up. Three large units cumulatively embrace a variety of habitats: riverbank, floodway, and floodplain; swamps and sloughs; cow farms and corn farms; and valley-wall forests.

Snoqualmie River near Crescent Lake

Crescent Lake (Two Rivers)

Round trip 2 miles, allow 2 hours
High point 32 feet, no elevation gain
All year (except during floodtime)

Only by boat can the Snoqualmie be closely inspected in this jungle-banked stretch, and the Skykomish is barricaded by a tangled wetland. So let the rivers be and poke about a floodway forest of the sort that once covered hundreds of square miles of Puget Sound lowlands but now is a rarity.

A path follows Crescent "Lake" easterly a bit and charmingly crosses this excellent slough on a plank bridge through lily pads and blackbirds and ducks. Walk north on a (sometimes) gated farm road between pasture and lake. In ½ mile the road, field, and lake end at a (sometimes) footbridge over the slough outlet. Awesome cedars and Sitka spruce. Splendid cottonwoods. Bigleaf maples, boughs arching and intertwining on high, dripping licorice fern. Riley Slough cries out for a raft to drift to—where? The map shows it draining into both the Snoqualmie and the Skykomish close above their confluence as the Snohomish River. Ought to be called *Three* Rivers.

Cherry Valley

Round trip 3 miles, allow 3 hours
High point 200 feet, elevation gain 160 feet

The floodplain bulges a green bay into the High Rock Hills, the fields pastoral-pleasing, the views broad, and the sky liberating.

The walking can begin from the two public accesses beside Highway 203 or a third 1.2 miles up Cherry Valley Road from the north edge of Duvall.

From the latter, elevation 40 feet, a 1-mile loop trail ascends hillside forest and traverses in and out of trickle-creek gulches.

From any of the accesses, a network of service roads and hunter-tramped paths leads every which way in the 386 acres of the Cherry Valley HMA to where Cherry Creek is pent between a dike and the valley wall. Skunk-cabbage swamp nourishes groves of big old spruce. Drainage ditches are thoroughfares for flitting and swimming birds; beware of pterodactyls lifting off in a fright of harsh croaks and gangly flappings. Footbridges cross the ditches at convenient intervals, marked by poles visible from afar. Look up to a surprising rock cliff and a startling column of white water in the trees—McCauley Falls.

Cherry Valley Unit, Snoqualmie Habitat Management Area

Stillwater

Introductory round trip 2 miles, allow 2 hours
High point 60 feet, no elevation gain

The public isn't generally invited to snoop around a farm because feet bother the crops or people bother the animals. (In England, public paths through farms are signed, "Do Not Worry the Sheep.") However, on the 450-acre Stillwater HMA the crops are secondary to recreation—indeed, some corn is treacherously planted to lure fowl into shotgun range so they can be re-created. In shooting season, pacifists ought to stay away. Most of the year, though, the floodplain quiet is disturbed only by sounds of river and birds.

Don't expect signs; the Wildlife Department is too starved for funds to afford amenities. The organized eaters of wildlife blame the growing shortage of eatables on the bureaucracy, as if it were the builder of housing tracts and shopping centers. In a less impoverished past, the Wildlife Department saved habitats by use of state appropriations, federal grants, and fees from hunting and fishing licenses. When federal funding was diverted to overseas gunnery, support was sought from a clientele that had grown to outnumber the critter-eaters—hikers and floaters and birders were required to purchase conservation licenses. But the agency couldn't afford staff to enforce the system and gave it up in despair. A state bond issue has revived the habitat-acquisition program. Still no money for amenities.

What's to be done in a tract ¾ of a square mile in area, with 2 miles of riverbank, a slough, two creeks, two ponds, cattail marshes, grasslands, brush, and farmland? Prowl around watching for birds and beasts; to quote the Wildlife Department brochure, there are pheasant, ducks, rabbit, snipe, mink, goldfinch, deer, and bear. Absorb the essence of the broad valley between forested highlands, look long and far to Si on the Cascade scarp.

For an introductory walk, start at the southern parking area and go north ¼ mile on Snoqualmie River Trail to a farm road leading out in the fields. Follow the lane as it climbs onto an old, mostly overgrown dike, drops off it, and after much wandering ends in 1 long mile at a tanglewood guarding a murky slough—Harris Creek. A slippery plank footbridge crosses the creek, a path winds through woods to a gravel bar on the Snoqualmie River. Wild! Remote!

Tolt River (MacDonald Memorial) Park
(Map—page 36)

Perimeter loop and sidetrips 4 miles, allow 3 hours
High point 450 feet, elevation gain 700 feet
All year

The size of this King County park, a "mere" 220 acres, belies the richness and variety of wildwoods and wild-river experiences on its miles (unbelievably many) of trails.

From the south edge of Carnation on Highway 203, drive west 0.3 mile on NE 40 Street to the parking lot, elevation 60 feet.

Pleasant car-camping sites are carved in the forest. Picnic tables are scattered about wide green fields under the big sky, inviting a romp in the sun to banks of the Snoqualmie River and downstream to banks of the Tolt River. (The confluence is the site of a village inhabited for centuries. The Tolt Historical Society proposes to change the name of

Footbridge over the Snoqualmie River at MacDonald Memorial Park

the park to the one applied to the site by the Original Residents.)

The crossing to the wild side of the Snoqualmie, the largest segment of the park, is alone worth the visit. The 500-foot swinging bridge (no jumping up and down, please, and troops please break step) was built as a Bicentennial project in 1976 by the 409th Engineering Company, Army Reserve, and leads to the hike-in campsites and the trail system. No precise recipe is required for the 10 miles (a guess) of built and just-happened paths. The following perimeter loop (with sidetrips) is a good introduction.

Cross the bridge, pausing to look upstream to Tiger Mountain and downstream to Three Fingers Mountain. On the far side turn right, downstream, on the trail signed "River Road." Taking time out for excursions to the riverbank, where ducks dabble and fish jump and gulls fly, proceed through pristine floodway forest of cottonwoods that are not terribly large, meaning the area was flooded to bare gravel in not too distant a past. The way enters a field and passes North Field Shelter, a large lean-to where in event of downpour the patrols can gather from tent sites tucked away in the woods.

In 1 mile is a Y, the left fork signed "Cottonwood Loop." Before doing that, take the right fork to big gravel bars, the end of the old road, and a path that skirts a deep-woods slough to a wide dike with broad views over river and valley.

Cottonwood Loop turns toward the valley wall, switchbacks up onto it, and turns upvalley, contouring at just enough distance above the floor to give the sensation of walking through treetops, looking down on the birds. Lookout Trail diverges steeply right, climbing to a ridge point at some 450 feet, with views to river, pastures, and the Cascades from Three Fingers to Sultan to Index to Si. Traversing over ribs and ravines, it climbs to still better views, then drops back to Cottonwood Loop. Another trail, signed "Railroad Grade" (from the days of "lokie" logging), joins in from the sloughs and mixed forest below and the way drops to fields of Orchard Camp, on the slopes above the swinging bridge.

Tolt Pipeline–Tolt River Forks–North Fork Gorge
(Map—page 55)

In past writings this surveyor has praised pedestrian pleasures in the Great Big Western Tree Farm, the sprawl of forests between the Cascade front and the Snoqualmie River. But it came to pass that whenever he returned to a favorite sylvan haunt he found it desylvanized. When he sought out a beloved old logging-railroad grade dwindled to a trail, it had been bulldozed and crush-rocked. The map of the "Marckworth Freeway" in the out-of-print *Footsore 2* tells how much good walking country has been lost. This book sadly concedes the GBWTF to workaday trucks and playday motor-rompers.

Most of it. By the great golly, not *all* of it! The Tolt River runs through it and so does the Tolt Pipeline of the Seattle Water Department, which polices the route to firmly exclude public motors from the pipeline (and thus, incidentally, the river) yet benignly tolerates law-abiding feet. Granted, the pipeline route is a wide gravel road. But quiet. And amid the enslaved tree-farm monotone are sparkling delights of free Nature.

Snoqualmie Valley to Harris Creek

Round trip 9 miles, allow 6 hours
High point 550 feet, elevation gain (going and coming) 1400 feet
All year

Stroll through second-growth by the occasional horse corral and cow pasture and stumpranch. Great fun on a winter day when the kids want to frolic in pretty snow but the family car is a-feared to venture off valley pavement up slippery hill roads.

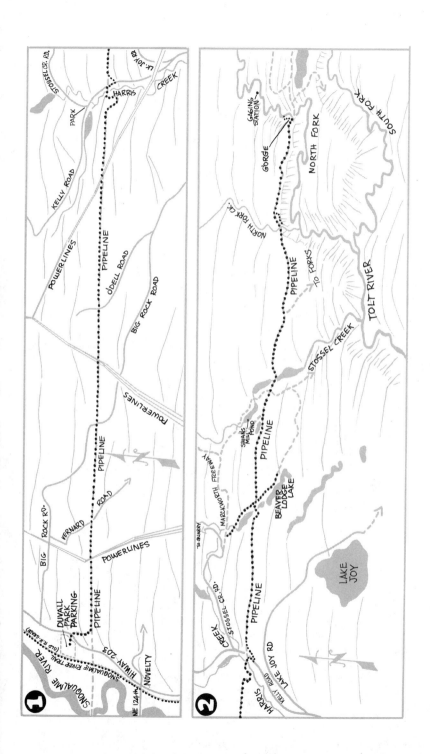

Drive Highway 203 to 1.5 miles south of Duvall and park at Duvall Park, elevation 80 feet.

Cross the highway to the Tolt River Headquarters and the gated service road, driven only by very occasional work vehicles and thus usually silent, most gratefully on Sundays when the rest of the GBWTF is a racket. The road slants up the valley wall to intersect the pipeline and runs a compass course due east, moderately up and down. Vernard Road is crossed, and Big Rock Road, and O'Dell Road, all accessible from Big Rock Road, which takes off from Highway 203 at ¼ mile north of Duvall Park. At 4½ miles the pipeline tops a rise with a view east to Tolt headwaters, then drops to Harris Creek and the pastures and homes of Kelly Road.

Harris Creek to North Fork Tolt River

Round trip (exclusive of sidetrips) 10 miles, allow 7 hours
High point 780 feet, elevation gain (going and coming) 1200 feet
All year

Habitations are left, tree farm entered, no more public roads crossed or neared. Second-growth alternates with third-growth plantations. Yawn. But the *sidetrips*—thereby hangs the tale.

From Stillwater Store on Highway 203, drive Stillwater Hill Road, signed "Lake Joy," 1.4 miles to a Y. Go right on Kelly Road 0.6 mile to another Y. Lake Joy Road goes left; keep right 1 mile to a third Y and park, elevation 336 feet.

Walk back down Kelly Road the short bit to the gated service road and climb it to the plateau rolling east to the mountain front.

Beaver Lodge Lake

At 1½ miles an obscure sideroad goes right ¼ mile to a lake ½ mile long, in flowering time a yellow brilliance of pond lily. Frogs croak. Ducks quack. Walk sunken logs to close views of the heaped-up brush of an abandoned beaver lodge. Binoculars may find the new headquarters. For sure, they're still around.

Swan's Mill Pond

At 2½ miles, having descended nearly to the bottom of Stossel Creek valley, the pipeline is joined on the left by a 1980s logging road and, a bit farther along, by the 1930s Swan Loop Road, both blocked against razzer invasions by large boulders. Sidetrip ⅓ mile on the Swan Loop Road to Swan's Mill Pond, 500 feet.

Paul Bunyan's great-grandson's cousin operated a mill here until about 1947, buying cutting rights from Weyerhaeuser and the state. The legend says he was careless about paying bills and workers, artfully exploited the bankruptcy laws, and threatened physical violence to children caught picking "his" wild blackberries. Having skinned the Tolt country and provoked so many enemies after his scalp that he couldn't walk the streets of Carnation without a loaded shotgun, he decamped for Oregon, where the Klamath Indians just had had their reservation terminated and were having their Ponderosa pine forests transferred to a band of freebooters who took this opportunity to compensate for having missed the Sand Creek Massacre. The story has it that the Oregon pickings were so rich that Bunyan's relative didn't even say goodbye to the Tolt, just walked away from the mill and ma-

Beaver house on Beaver Lodge Lake

chinery and unpaid payroll, the miles of railroad track, and the locomotives. Creditors salvaged what they could, scavengers gleaned, and
the only traces of the epic picaresque now to be seen are some big tim-
bers, rusty junk, and the dam and pond.

Tolt River Forks

At 3 miles, a long ½ mile past the sideroad to Swan's Mill Pond and
very near the crest of the ascent from the marshy bottom of Stossel
Creek, a path angles off right, directly across from a yellow post
marked "RW MON 371+9019." This is the resumption, such as it is, of
the old Swan Loop Road. In a long ½ mile from the pipeline, elevation
720 feet, it turns right to the Tolt scarp and in another ½ mile south
dives off the brink, narrowing to a trail that in a steep ¼ mile ends on a
bluff immediately above the forks. Elevation at the river, 360 feet.

In olden days the small flat of the bluff, now grown up in brush,
was a well-stomped camp where Boy Scouts learned to cook kabob and
mulligan, build a bough bed and shiver all night in a rain-soaked wool
blanket, and sing marching songs while dying (or nearly) of a condition
that years later was dignified as "hypothermia." Much has happened
to the countryside over the years, but so vigorous and swift is the
growth of the green at this elevation of Western Washington that sur-
veys of the late 1970s and middle 1980s found the scene amazingly
little changed from the 1930s and just as exciting—to an old Boy Scout,
anyhow.

Three things must be done. First, walk paths out atop short cliffs
falling to the river, which just here at the union of the forks slips between rock-wall portals. Second, scramble down to the gravel bar, assume the costume, and plunge into the Ol' Swimmin' Hole. Third,
follow the trail ½ mile downstream past the gaging station to Stossel
Creek and its joyous camp in the grove of giant cottonwoods.

North Fork Gorge

At 5 miles the pipeline crosses the North Fork. From the bridge
look down a hundred-odd feet. Quail. The river, which in most of its
course westward is sliced in glacial rubble, here is slotted in hard rock,
squeezed to a width of barely 6 feet, the water a deafening white boil.
Just short of the bridge, find the path down through the woods to pot-
holes up to 6 feet wide and 8 feet deep, scoured in the sandstone by
floodwater-swirled boulders. The river seems narrow enough for a jump.

North Fork Gorge

Tolt River Trail
(Map—page 60)

This here surveyor commenced his trail surveying in 1937 on the Tolt River, which was as far from home as Troop 324 could get its fathers to drive them during the Great Depression. The river trail began in Carnation, but we intersected it on a feeder path from Moss "Lake," then only recently been made so by a peatmoss mine. The feeder took us some ¾ mile through a recent clearcut to the brink of the glacial-debris plateau, elevation 500 feet, and skidded a scant ¼ mile down the gravel-sand-clay to virgin forest on a river terrace at 300 feet. At the upstream end of the terrace, the river trail skinnied by a stretch where the Tolt was cutting into the scarp, forcing a climb above clay muck, followed by a descent to Stossel Creek, reached at 1 mile from the Moss Lake cutoff. A cedar bridge crossed to a cedar-plank cabin, moss-hung apple trees, and forget-me-nots blooming in a garden long left to its own devices. A final ½ mile took us to the Ol' Swimmin' Hole at the Tolt Forks.

The trail was resurveyed repeatedly until 1940, then given up in favor of the remote wilderness of the Olympics and Cascades. In the

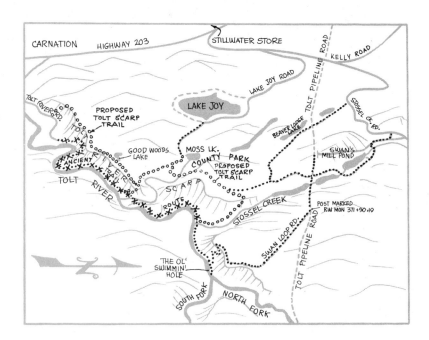

Fungus growing on a tree along the Tolt River

1970s the surveyor was smitten by a vision, was commanded by Higher (or Lower?) Powers to explore and catalog and describe in a book "the wildness within." *Footsore* had several beginnings. Puget Sound beaches. Issaquah Alps. The Ol' Swimmin' Hole....

Scouting trips culminated in the full-scale expedition of late summer 1977. The river trail had been replaced for the 4 miles from Carnation by Entwistle Street–Tolt River Road, ending at 240 feet. A fishermen's scramble path clambered to 400 feet, near the scarp top, and skidded to a river terrace, its virgin forest only recently clearcut. The walking was easy on bits of path and cat road, then gravel bars. Where the river cut the scarp, the surveyor took to the river for some ½ mile of knee-deep wading through rapids. A brief surcease from blue knees came at the expedition climax, moss-green twilight of ancient cedar-spruce forest protected from loggers by the mean terrain. Old old campsites on narrow benches in purely primeval wilderness poignantly recalled the condition of the entire Tolt canyon in 1937.

More wading, more new clearcut on the terrace of the Moss Lake junction. At terrace's end the tread of the old trail was clearly defined, though long unused, as it plunged into a splendid forest of big firs and cedars. Again a slope of mobile blue clay, again into the river, surprising a doe and two fawns. Wildlife! Wild river! Blue knees! Numb feet! Again onto land, again old tread. The remains of two bridges over Stossel Creek, the site of the vanished cabin. The magnificent camp on a sandy beach under spreading boughs of cedars and cottonwoods. The loggers had not (yet) descended into the canyon to this and other "long corners." The forest of 1977 was that of 1937. On the Tolt there still was wildness within!

A final ½ mile on good trail. The gravel bar where the North Fork and South Fork united in a wide, deep, languid flow of limeade before the whitewater tumble through the rock at the portals, elevation 360 feet. Having been 4 hours under way in the hot summer sun, the surveyor was pleased in his lordly solitude to assume the costume.

So it was in 1977 and on resurveys of the 1980s. The surveyor heard rumors that King County Parks was talking about a Tolt River Trail. Queries substantiated the expected: sitting at desks, scanning maps, they had no idea what they were talking about. But the surveyor talked to local folks who did. Something may come of it.

A river trail as of old would be formidably expensive to build and maintain and probably ecologically unwise. The riverbanks may best remain a pure wildland, secure from any additional logging but also from throngs of boots. A human (foot-only) presence would appear compatible with wildlife habitat at the Moss Lake Cutoff Terrace and the trail from Tolt Forks to Stossel Creek.

A scarp trail is more feasible. At ½ mile before the end of Tolt River Road, switchbacks could climb a powerline swath from a trailhead at 230 feet to the scarp rim at 580 feet. Brushed-over logging roads and cat tracks readily could be opened for feet the 1½ miles to "Good Woods Lake," whose shoreline forest of old cedars was spared in the 1930s by clearcutters because it was a favorite fishing hole and again in the 1970s because the Wildlife Department insisted.

A scant ½ mile more would intersect the route of the old Moss Lake Cutoff. The deep ravine of Moss Lake's outlet would force the way ½ mile inland to 350-acre Moss Lake County Park and the peatbog interpretive center envisioned for what King County Parks has hailed as its "Number One Wetland." A relocated ½-mile path down the Tolt scarp would permit human visits to the river terrace; the cruel terrain upstream and downstream from the terrace would guarantee that feet would not invade wildlife privacy.

In a long 1 mile or so from Moss Lake, the way would climb to a 600-foot plateau and drop steeply to cross Stossel Creek near its mouth, 350 feet, to the existing ½-mile trail to the forks. Deadend here! Let the gorges of both forks be left to the wildness which is deeper than

Tolt River

most of most national parks. (In 1940 the surveyor, trapped in a maze of fresh logging slash, escaped by wading a number of miles down the South Fork to the Forks. Blue knees! But good! In the 1980s he followed abandoned logging roads to the South Fork at several points. The wading looked as superior as ever.)

This prospective scarp route, as well as the river-level route done by the surveyor in 1977, are quite possible now. But you really gotta want it. Returning in the late 1980s, the surveyor inspected the situation carefully, thought it over, and took the Tolt Pipeline route to the Ol' Swimmin' Hole.

Issaquah–North Bend Trail
(Map—page 65)

One way from Issaquah to North Bend 15 (or 20?) miles, allow all day
High point 500 feet, elevation gain 500 feet
All year
Bus: Metro 210

On the Fourth of July of 1890, Daniel Gilman celebrated completion of his railway from Seattle to Woodinville to Issaquah (which gratefully, if temporarily, changed its name to "Gilman") to Snoqualmie Falls by running an excursion train to the falls. The line, completed later that year to Sallal Prairie, east of North Bend, hauled to Seattle the coal from Issaquah mines and the produce from a farmland whose prosperity is suggested by the fact that in a single year the trains killed 198 farm animals. In the 1920s passenger service was discontinued, and several decades later the Northern Pacific, which had swallowed up Gilman, stopped the trains altogether.

King County Parks employed Forward Thrust bond funds to acquire the grade from Preston to Snoqualmie Falls. The State Highway Department bought the route west to Issaquah. As of 1994 these and several other bureaucracies are milling around.

Issaquah to High Point

Round trip 5 miles, allow 4 hours
High point 450 feet, elevation gain 350 feet

Though title has not yet been conveyed, as promised, to King County Parks and the trail has no official existence, it has been continuously open to the feet since 1890.

Go off I-90 on Exit 17, drive Front Street south to Sunset Way, turn left to where Sunset is about to become an on-ramp to I-90, and park on nearby residential streets, elevation 100 feet.

A divider-protected walkway on the north side of Sunset leads to an official City of Issaquah trail sign, "Snoqualmie Falls." The trail passes through an open-gate fence to East Fork Issaquah Creek. A bridge built by the Chief Ranger of the Issaquah Alps Trails Club crosses to a grassy slope beyond the freeway underpass and a climb to the rail grade, attained at 250 feet, a scant ¼ mile from Sunset.

The 2¼ miles to High Point are the happiest of strolling. No hills to huff up. No brush to soak the socks. Cool breezes in the shadowed ravines

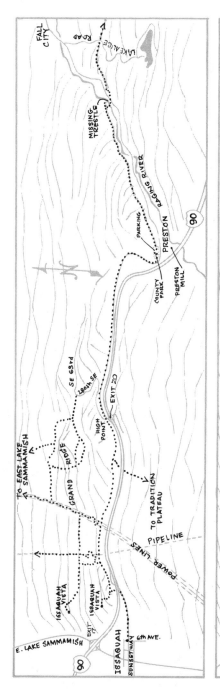

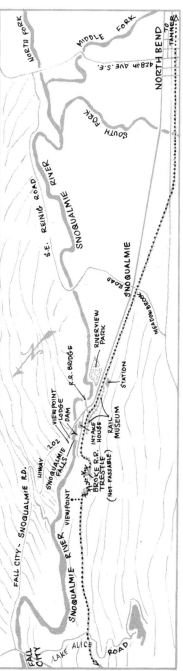

Issaquah to Preston trail near Issaquah

of tumbling creeks. Off the west end of the grade, where the trestle used to cross high above East Fork, a path to Issaquah Vista and wide-angle views over the city, the Issaquah Alps, and Lake Sammamish. Somewhat to the east, a path under the thundering 1980s freeway to a quiet (long abandoned) 1920s bridge of old Sunset Highway, and a climb to Tradition Plateau. Paths down to the East Fork, whose gravels are the spawning grounds of races of wild salmon which have only the most distant cousinship to the tame salmon of the Issaquah Fish Hatchery, the pests that have driven the natives out of the South Fork. Artifacts of an old coal mine. The second-largest glacial erratic in the Issaquah Alps. The Flower Wall, a lava cliff displaying some of the prettiest of the hundred species that bloom along the trail in spring. A path to the Monster Fir, patriarch of a grove of ancient forest. Powerlines and gas lines, in themselves a bore, which ascend Grand Ridge to square miles of controversy between the Greens and the Grays.

High Point is an equally popular start for this walk, whose fame has yet to catch the attention of government. Go off I-90 on Exit 20 to Preston Way, and immediately past the interchange turn off to a parking space on the rail grade, elevation 450 feet.

High Point to Preston

Round trip 6 miles, allow 4 hours
High point 500 feet, elevation gain 50 feet

When the Highway Department was converting U.S. 10 to I-90, we worried about the rail trail walked since 1890. Olympia responded by despatching a Designated Sweet-Talker. He toured with us and at each point of our concern turned to his aide and said, "Make a note of that, Bottomley." Bottomley and the DST carried a sheaf of notes back to Olympia and we were blithe. Subsequently, monster machines seemed to be breaking the promises of the DST. We appealed to him in Olympia. He wasn't there. He wasn't nowhere. Olympia never had heard of Bottomley's notes. Thus began our education in how much faith to place in the DSTs of highwaymen (and land developers and, as far as that goes, certain parks departments).

Little old Preston Way, a remnant of Sunset Highway, carries scarcely more traffic than in the 1920s. Pleasant walking for nostalgic historicals. A delightful bikeway—and at ¼ mile short of Preston begins the official King County Parks pavement. Eventually a *foot* route must be restored; a portion of the grade survives in a jungle of hellberries.

For a unique outing, ride the Metro 210 from Issaquah to Preston and walk back to Issaquah. Better yet, take the 210 from Bellevue, Mercer Island, or Seattle, do the walk one-way or round-trip, and dispense with a private vehicle altogether.

Preston to Lake Alice Road

Round trip 7 miles, allow 4 hours
High point 500 feet, elevation gain 300 feet

Forests and creeks, flowers and birds and views, the peace of a motor-free day.

Go off I-90 on Exit 22 and drive the short bit east past Preston Mill ("Since 1896") to Preston County Park, elevation 500 feet. A staircase ascends past the community hall (more history, built by the Civilian Conservation Corps of song and story) to intersect the trail. We call it a "trail," though "bikeway" is more appropriate. King County Parks thinks that walking is supposed to be done on sidewalks and therefore whenever an old, informal, cherished trail is officially "improved," the blacktop cometh.

Houses of a hamlet that has grown gracefully into the forest yield to wildland on slopes above the Raging River. A waterfall invites a pause to enjoy the babble and suck in water-cooled air. A powerline suggests a long exploration to golly knows what and where on Mitchell Hill. An ancient woods road become game trail climbs to the top of a quarry—stay clear!

At 2 miles a much-loved timber trestle used to cross high above the Raging River. King County had funds allocated to buy the historical artifact. The railroad fully knew the public intent. But a gypo logger came by, free enterprise made a deal, and the public screamed in outrage, awaking King County Parks from its nap—too late. The railroad was so pleased by the manner in which it had adhered to the famous nineteenth-century dictum of Commodore Vanderbilt that when a

Issaquah–North Bend Bikeway near Preston; before paving, it was a foot / horse trail

high-flier from Montana jetted to Seattle it sold him the long-intended and well-publicized extension of the Burke-Gilman Trail west from Lake Union to Ballard.

Where the trestle used to be, the trail switchbacks down to Preston–Fall City Highway, dodges speeding vehicles to the far side, follows a motor-free ¼ mile of former highway, and switchbacks up to the grade. Pause to enjoy the Raging River, Seattle's closest "mountain river," though really just a creek except when it's raging.

The trail rounds a wooded corner from the valley of the Raging to that of the Snoqualmie. At 3½ miles is a parking area at the crossing of Lake Alice Road, 380 feet. This is the site of the Fall City Siding of the Northern Pacific; across the valley was the Fall City Siding of the Milwaukee line. (For a time Fall City occasionally had steamboats, too.)

Lake Alice Road to Snoqualmie Falls Vista

Round trip 3½ miles, allow 2 hours
High point 500 feet, elevation gain 120 feet

More forest. More blacktop. A view.

Drive 3 miles from Preston Mill on Preston–Fall City Highway and turn right on Lake Alice Road 0.8 mile to the Fall City Siding. The sign at the parking area warns, "Trail ends at Snoqualmie Falls Vista 1.8 miles. No outlet. Round trip only."

Beyond suburbia's gauntlet of power mowers and barking dogs, the quiet reclaims. Gulches are crossed on fills and trestles. A powerline horse trail is the gateway to miles of roaming on Lake Alice Plateau (aka Snoqualmie Ridge). Ruins of an old farm set a walker to elegizing. The knoll at the endpoint looks over valley pastures to Snoqualmie Falls and Mount Si.

Snoqualmie Falls Vista to Snoqualmie Falls

When hoboes were hopping the Gilman rails, this was a 1-mile walk. The distance is still that for feathered bipeds. What it ultimately will be for featherless bipeds is murky.

King County Parks bought the right-of-way, including the trestles. The very long one at the "Vista" was shorn of ties to protect adventurers from their own daring. A shorter one close to the falls was pulled down. By whom? With or without King County knowledge? Doughty hikers pioneered bypasses, expecting to see them tidied up by Parks. But though the county had bought the trestles—the air rights—ownership of the land beneath the trestles remained with Weyerhaeuser and

Puget Power, and for undeclared reasons they don't want the public to cross their property here.

Bypass routes exist and one or the other is likely to become "official," some 3 to 4 miles in length and largely on sidewalks of a New City planned for Snoqualmie Ridge.

Snoqualmie Falls

In 1991 Puget Sound Power and Light applied to the Federal Energy Regulatory Commission for a 40-year relicense to continue use of Snoqualmie Falls. The published application to the federals spells out an expanded exploitation that would entail manipulation of the landscape and river. Objections have been made by the Snoqualmie people, supported by Christian church groups and environmental organizations. At issue are (1) the proposed expansion; (2) the propriety of the existing use; (3) whether it is true that the Snoqualmies have considered the falls sacred for millennia; (4) whether the Snoqualmie people exist as such, not having been signatory to the "treaties" of the midnineteenth century (in May 1993, the federals ruled that the Snoqualmies do indeed exist); and (5) peripherally, a bunch of other things, such as adjacent real estate developments planned by Puget Power and Weyerhaeuser.

The Mountains to Sound Greenway may be described, in its present stage, as a backbone connecting head bone, leg bones, arm bones, finger bones, and toe bones. Were Greenwayites to start scuffling over details of the bonery, the odds are they'd end up breaking the backbone. The strategy, therefore, is to proceed on the basis of areas of unanimity, leaving the scuffling, if any, to other arenas. The Snoqualmie Falls dispute is between two groups of Greenwayites. This book is dedicated first off to supporting the young and tender backbone and therefore will not argue either case. The interested reader is sure to be kept fully informed by the public press.

The waters and the riverbed are public property, and the company thus must prove its use of them serves the public interest, primarily by supplying power at reasonable rates. However, recent amendments to federal law require that the public be additionally compensated for free use of its water. "Amelioration" must be provided.

The best we can do for a pedestrian here is send him/her to Puget Power's "amelioration" Snoqualmie Falls Park, new name for a spectacle that for a century has been outranked in visitor popularity in the state only by Mount Rainier. An observation platform juts into space 300 feet above the plunge basin. A nature trail descends through big old trees to Powerhouse No. 2, built in 1910, for views from below.

Snoqualmie Falls from trail behind powerhouse

Come in midweek during the winter monsoon. You can then get a parking place. Moreover, what with the floodwater, there likely will actually be, then, a veritable Snoqualmie Falls.

A route over private property used to be open to the public on the wild side of the river, through the mist forest to the plunge basin and the tailrace discharge tunnel of Powerhouse No. 1, built in 1898, entirely underground, a feat that set Seattle newspapers to gaping.

In 1946 the surveyor first walked through the mist forest of lichen-silvery alders, moss-swollen maples, and hemlocks growing 100 feet up from cedar nurse-stumps. At the plunge basin he watched a billow of mist roll his way—and when the "mist" arrived was pounded to the ground by tons of floodwater. He liked it so well he returned often and in 1977 wrote it up for *Footsore 2*. Fourteen years after publication he received an angry (if tardy) phone call from a member of the family that owns the access to the mist forest and suddenly did not wish to share it.

The recommended action, of course, is for the public to purchase the mist-forest trail. Until that happens, those questing the millennia-old religious experience must emulate the early Christians. To be kept in mind is what happened when those worshippers came up out of the catacombs and met the lions. In 1992 the surveyor drove the public David Powell Road to make sure the private drive to Snoqualmie Falls Forest Theater (and mist forest) was adequately signed "No Trespassing." As he was reading the signs, a car passed and the driver glowered. He must have got himself instantly to a phone to call 911 because as the surveyor was standing on the public road admiring the river a police car came a-howling. Don't mess around on David Powell Road.

Snoqualmie

Round trip 2 miles, allow 2 hours
High point 420 feet, no elevation gain

"Hop Farm" it was known as when Gilman steamed onto the scene. The largest hop farm in the world. No more hops, but still plenty of history, partly because the town is periodically in the Snoqualmie River. Even when the river is flowing within its banks, the town is inseparable from the river and its falls. The falls are the proper start for a walk through time. Puget's Snoqualmie Falls Park is the west end, but on busy days the falls are best visited from a parking place in or near town, on the east. However, though the rail trail from Issaquah is missing a crucial mile, it can be walked from the east nearly to the gap.

Drive Highway 202 for 0.5 mile east of Snoqualmie Falls Park, and just across the river bridge reverse-turn west on Powerhouse Road. Park on a shoulder, elevation 420 feet.

Walk the railway, which here has rails and ties. In the 0.2 mile west to the (intact) Snoqualmie Falls Station are close looks at turn-of-the-century masonry in buildings of the Powerhouse No. 1 complex, cross-river views to the lordly lodge rising haughtily high above the brink of the falls. The rails proceed into fine, ferny forest with views out to the valley downstream of the falls, past a precipice where a fence prevents falling into the falls or even seeing them. A fence across the tracks prevents progress to the cliff where architects are sketching—well, who knows?

Now, eastward. Exactly where Powerhouse Road turns off the highway, spot the start of Snoqualmie Centennial Corridor Trail/Bikeway. Take a squint at the woods on the far side of Highway 202 to find the railroad spur that bridges the river, former connection of the Northern Pacific and the Milwaukee, competitors for output of the Weyerhaeuser mill. Farther along, in town, sidestreet stubs end at riverbank parks.

The center ring of the Snoqualmie show is the living railroad. The trail parallels the tracks where the Puget Sound Railway Historical Association exhibits a dozen steam locomotives, a diesel, and rolling stock (coaches, cabooses, snowplows, crane), the largest collection west of the Mississippi. In 0.7 mile from Snoqualmie Falls Station is Snoqualmie Depot, built by Messrs. Burke and Gilman in 1890, now housing the historical museum of Railroad Place Park.

Puget Sound & Snoqualmie Valley Railroad

Snoqualmie Depot is the parking place of a real live steam locomotive and attached train of coaches. On weekends, holidays, and some ordinary days, it awakes to choo-chooing and whistling exuberance as the Puget Sound Railway Historical Association conducts a 2-hour, 6-mile round trip to North Bend and tracks-end at Ballarat Avenue, to which spot the depot built in 1886 at Lester on the Northern Pacific mainline recently was moved.

The train and depots are spiffied up to Gay Nineties appearance, as are the volunteers who operate the trains, garbed in period mustaches and dress.

The 3 miles between the depots are open to walking, of course, and excellently nostalgic for old hoboes who as children grew up matching lengths of steps to the tie spacing and holding one-on-one, side-by-side contests to see who was best at walking rails. For just plain and ordi-

Snoqualmie Depot museum

nary pedestrianism, the Milwaukee line across the river is better. The fun here is the rail trip. Take the Metro 210 bus from Seattle, ride the train to North Bend and back, tour the museums, wet your whistle at a table in the open-air garden of refreshment, and return to the city having spent an entire day free of your automobile.

The grade (no rails, no ties) continues intact east past Ballarat Avenue a scant 2 miles as a path beside North Bend Way (old U.S. 10) to Tanner Road and the junction with the Milwaukee. A person could walk from here to Issaquah (or for that matter, Ballard, terminus of Gilman's Seattle, Lakeshore & Eastern). He/she could walk east, via the Milwaukee, to the Cascade Crest and Chicago, Milwaukee, and St. Paul.

Three Forks Regional Wildlife Park/Refuge
(Map—page 75)

Allow an hour or all day
High point 440 feet
All year (except during floodtime)
Bus: Metro 210

In an age when scarcely a flat acre west of the Cascades is not hungrily eyed for houses, shopping centers, golf courses, soccer fields, or gridlockways, a substantial Snoqualmie–North Bend bottomland is conceded to the birds. That's because it's only part-time land. Within a long ½ mile (as the corvid flies, much more as the water flows), the three forks of the Snoqualmie River unite, and when one isn't flooding, another one or two are and often all three at once.

During the frontier era when the continent's short-grass prairies were being plowed, the soil then blowing on the wind to dirty the air of New York City, and the Old Settler of Puget Sound was burning the thousand-year-old trees off his homestead, confidently expecting to grow corn to size, floodplains looked like money in the bank. Some third-generation families remain on the land (and the water), and if they've never made money, they've grown food—how many airplane mechanics and computer programmers can make that claim? Love of home is not to be dismissed for the public convenience. The Greens will be pleased to see the farmers stay. The more farms the better. The Greens do support a policy of buying development rights from willing sellers or, if preferred by the owner, fee title, giving life-tenancy to the

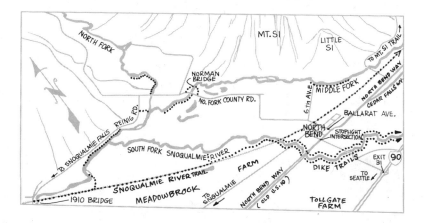

Norman Bridge and Mount Si

sellers. But the Greens are not fully enamored of the public relations of King County Parks, nor do they swallow with a smile the county plans. The Holly Farm would become a parking lot. Has the wildlife been consulted about the trail projected for the full length of the park?

The county (and state, and the municipalities of Snoqualmie and North Bend) plan a 400-acre Three Forks Regional Wildlife Park/Refuge encompassing the mouths of the three forks, the half-mile between, and lands downstream from the mouth of the South Fork to Reinig Bridge on the united river. No playfields, no campgrounds. Nevertheless, the vision must be criticized as too small. The scene calls for a super-park encompassing the three forks, Meadowbrook Farm, and Tollgate—and for maintaining much of the park in working farms.

Humans only will know this park intimately from a kayak or canoe or raft, but pedestrians will have a crack at the riverbanks, floodway forests, and sloughs. Six samplings are suggested.

For openers, see "Snoqualmie River Trail," described earlier in these pages. Drive from Snoqualmie to Reinig (railroad) Bridge, and park on the shoulder, elevation 400 feet. Walk across the bridge and over Meadowbrook Farm 1¼ miles to Mt. Si Golf Course.

From the bridge, drive (pausing to train binoculars on the sloughs) Reinig Road 1 mile, to where it returns to the river, and park on the shoulder. Across the river the South Fork emerges from the largest of Three Forks wet jungles. Wish for a kayak to get in there. In the lack, walk the road upstream to gravel bars.

From the confluence drive Reinig Road 0.5 mile, to about 0.3 mile short of North Fork County Road. Look sharp for a cable-barred, overgrown woods road. Park on the shoulder. The lane penetrates a grove of glorious maples to a huge gravel bar at the confluence of the North and Middle Forks.

Turn south from Reinig Road on North Fork County Road 0.2 mile to the North Fork bridge. Park. Walk the north-side dike upstream about ½ mile to its end, then continue on gravel bars.

From the North Fork bridge, drive North Fork County Road 0.4 mile to the Middle Fork bridge. The old Norman Bridge, last timber-truss vehicle bridge in King County, has been preserved as a pedestrian-only King County Landmark. Park on the shoulder just south of the new bridge. A lane enters floodway forest and in ⅓ mile of cottonwoods ends at the river. A bit south, past a cattail pond, is a large bar in close view of the North Fork confluence.

Again refer to "Snoqualmie River Trail." Park on Main Avenue at the west edge of North Bend. Just beyond the South Fork bridge, leave the trail on a path to sprawling bars, some of them gravel, some of them sand ideal for castles. Farther along the grade another path cuts through floodway forest to the river and more bars. Watch for tooth-logging and beaver-engineering. No trophy of a Sunday walk is more treasured by kids than a "beaver stick." Adult cameras will come home with dozens of shots of the 3500-foot scarp of Mount Si, full face and profile, framed by railroad bridge and cottonwood forest, foregrounded by pasture and river, bright in morning sun and brooding in evening shadows.

South Fork Dikes
(Map—page 79)

Total length of all dikes 9 miles, allow 1 to 12 hours
High point 480 feet, next to no elevation gain
All year
Bus: Metro 210

Granted, a channelized and diked and riprapped river is a drainage ditch, kissing cousin to Metro's trunk sewer to West Point. However, the water flows in the open, rippling and rattling, and doesn't smell bad. Fish swim and fisherbirds fly and dive. The flat and easy walking along the dikes is enlivened by the Wagnerian omnipresence of Mount Si. The walker who views the dikes as ho-hum trails may be additionally stimulated by reflections on why the dikes exist and make plans to return when the river reprises its wild past.

Dikes go downstream from North Bend's Gardner Weeks Memorial Park 1 mile, through the west edge of town and under old U.S. 10, and the older Sunset Highway, and the still older Gilman and Milwaukee railways—a museum of transportation history displaying (counting the I-90 bridge, upstream from here) a century of bridge technology, the start closer to the youth of the Industrial Revolution than to our own time.

Dikes go upstream on both banks, that on the true right (the right side of the river when facing the direction of flow) all the way to Cedar Falls Road—2¼ air miles, 3 miles as the river goes. (It has been channelized but not straightened.) That on the true left stops short, a cliff obviating the need for a dike. Both pass under the I-90 bridge, evidencing how far man has advanced since the horse and buggy, choo-choo, and Model T, paralleling his progress from gunpowder to TNT to the H-bomb.

To start from the west, go off I-90 on Exit 31 and drive North Bend Boulevard to a block short of North Bend Way, the town's main drag (old U.S. 10), and park at Gardner Weeks Memorial Park, location of Snoqualmie Valley Museum and Mt. Si Senior Center, elevation 440 feet. Some accesses to the dikes hereabouts may be posted; if so, choose another from among the many available. (The dikes serve the populace as public walkways.)

To start from the east, go off I-90 on Exit 32 to 436th (Cedar Falls Road), drive to the river bridge, park on either side of the bridge, and

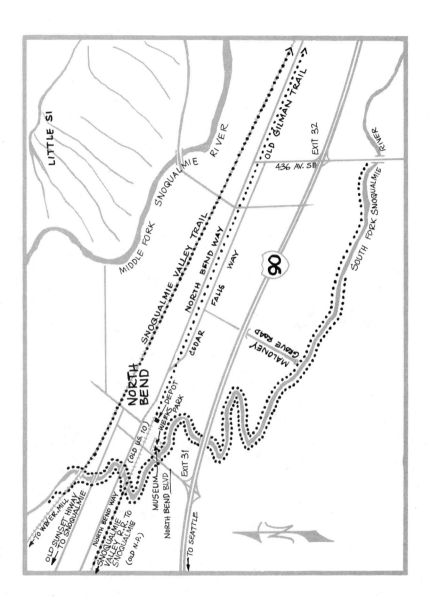

LITTLE SI

MIDDLE FORK SNOQUALMIE RIVER

OLD GILMAN TRAIL

EXIT 32

436 AV. SE

SNOQUALMIE VALLEY TRAIL

NORTH BEND WAY

FALLS WAY

90

SOUTH FORK SNOQUALMIE RIVER

NORTH BEND

CEDAR

MALONEY GROVE ROAD

(OLD US. 10)

WEEKS DEPOT PARK

MUSEUM

EXIT 31

NORTH BEND BLVD

TO WBLER.MILL

OLD SUNSET HWAY TO SNOQUALMIE

NORTH BEND WAY

SNOQUALMIE VALLEY R.R. TO SNOQUALMIE (OLD N.P.)

TO SEATTLE

Mount Si from South Fork Snoqualmie River dike

get on the true right dike. (On the true left a gated road drops to a pleasant picnic spot by the water.)

To start at a historically fascinating midpoint, from North Bend drive east on Cedar Falls Way (the south half of old U.S. 10) 0.4 mile from its split-off from North Bend Way and turn right on Maloney Grove Road 1 mile to the underpass of I-90 and the road-end turn-

around at the dike. In the 1920s and 1930s, Maloney's Grove was famous throughout the region. America's new freedom of the wheels let
city folk roam way out here in the country, miles beyond even Snoqualmie Falls, but the wheels were not fast or dependable enough that
a drive to Snoqualmie Pass was less than an expedition. Maloney's
Grove was just right. Daddy would set up the wall tent and build a
campfire and then go fishing. Mother would do pancakes in morning
and weenies and beans at night (and between, go fishing). For the
dominant population there were swings and teeter-totters and chute-
the-chutes, a whirlagig merry-go-round powered by children, each
with one foot on the circle of planks, the other pushing off the ground,
and a cable slideway where a kid was pulley-hoisted in a seat high
from the Earth and set loose to whiz through the Sky faster than a
speeding bullet. Bang the drum slowly. Had Maloney's Grove not been
killed by better cars and highways, it never could have survived the
age of liability insurance.

The dikes are at their best (well, except for floodtime) on a spring
day when the intent on leaving the city is to hike high, and upon reaching North Bend the peaks are seen to be white to their very bottoms.
The views then are particularly dazzling over the bed of the Pleistocene lake to Rattlesnake, Washington, Mailbox/Garcia, valleys of
South Fork and Middle Fork, and inescapable Si. Especially for a person who has been spending a lot of time in the deep woods, the abundance of air and bigness of sky are exhilarating.

Mount Si Natural Resources Conservation Area

USGS maps: Snoqualmie, North Bend, Snoqualmie Lake
Green Trails maps: Bandera, Mount Si, Snoqualmie Pass

Had Nature installed Mount Si anywhere east of the Rocky Mountains, chances are it would have been America's first national park. Immigrants fresh off the boat from Europe hardly could have failed to accord the awesome upthrust the same respect as that of the Original Residents, domiciled in Western Washington ten or a dozen millennia. Any new arrival could plainly see that the mountain and the nearby falls were designated spots to listen attentively to the spirits of the sky. However, the competition among listening posts was fierce, and what brought in magazine writers and tourist dollars was volcanoes; Rainier/Tahoma was The Mountain fated to become the first national park outside Wyoming and California.

Nevertheless, if Si suffered from being commonplace, forever in the face of the local folks, the same could be said of potatoes, which the masses always rate their top vegetable. In 1977 the legislature finally respected the wishes of the masses and authorized the state Department of Natural Resources (DNR) to manage 2360 acres as the Mount Si Conservation Area. Though toothlessly vague, the legislation was sufficiently strong to let the DNR treat the peak as something special. In 1986 the legislature adopted a measure with excellent teeth, almost a state version of the National Wilderness Act. Under the new designation of Natural Resources Conservation Area (NRCA), resource extraction is virtually excluded in favor of wildlife habitat, gene-pool reserves, water quality, landscape preservation, education, research, and *low-impact* (note the emphasis—the words are specific in the legislation) recreation; natural ecosystems take precedence over every anthropocentric exploitation, not excluding fun and games.

As of 1993 the Mount Si NRCA, one of twenty-one embodiments of the new concept (a companion on the Greenway is the West Tiger Mountain NRCA), had been enlarged by transfers among DNR-managed trust lands and by an exchange for 2350 Weyerhaeuser acres, bringing the total to 7000 acres, 11 square miles, well along toward a projected

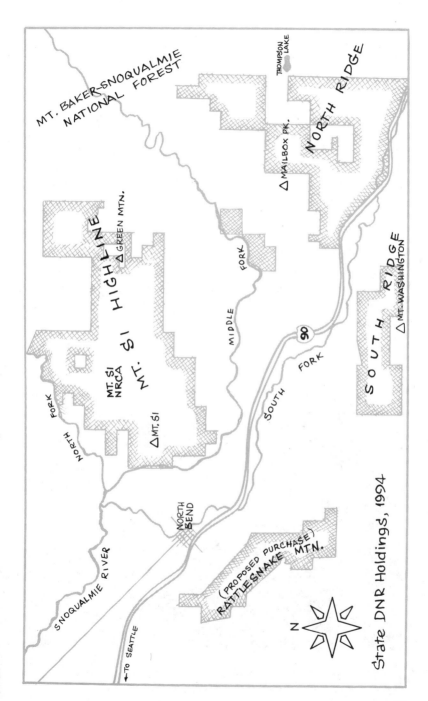

MT. BAKER-SNOQUALMIE NATIONAL FOREST

THOMPSON LAKE

NORTH RIDGE

△ MAILBOX PK.

△ GREEN MTN.

MT. SI HIGHLINE

MIDDLE FORK

SOUTH RIDGE

△ MT. WASHINGTON

90

MT. SI NRCA

MT. SI

△ MT. SI

SOUTH FORK

NORTH FORK

NORTH BEND

SNOQUALMIE RIVER

← TO SEATTLE

(PROPOSED PURCHASE)
RATTLESNAKE MTN.

N

State DNR Holdings, 1994

83

10,000 acres, nearly 16 square miles. Part will be "new wilderness" ("reclaimed" or "re-created"), where logging on high-elevation "tree farms" (actually, cellulose mines) has flushed so much soil down the streams that another "crop" could not grow in less than a millennium. Part will be genuine pristine wilderness, where cliffs have protected ancient forests from saws. In both old and new, the crush of commerce and heavy recreation will yield to the light-and-quiet *low-impact* recreations that accept the primacy of wild plants and creatures and waters and rocks.

As of 1994 the Mount Si NRCA extends from the banks of the North and Middle Forks Snoqualmie through Little Si to Big Si, Teneriffe, and Green. More is to come. A Mount Si Highline Trail on or near the summit ridge from Si to Teneriffe-Green-Moolock-Bessemer-Quartz. Views broad and long. Linkages to access trails from the valleys. Backcountry trail camps. As population pressures force use limits and a permit system in the Alpine Lakes Wilderness, the overflow of hikers will not be sent back to the city empty. On the Cascade edge they will find day-walk and backpack alternatives in terrain as pleasing as the spirit could wish yet in most part tough enough to withstand foot-trampling—and much of it open to ski-free feet in all those dreary months when the mountain interior is a wasteland of white slop.

Rocky outcrop at trail's end on Mount Si, overlooking Snoqualmie valley

Fuller Country
(Map—page 85)

Northeasterly of Mount Si, on high slopes of the Cascade front, forests have been clearcut to the last twig in the Great Big Western Tree Mine, where a successor to the crop Nature had been tending a dozen thousand years will not grow to mill size for so long that forest science will have time to catch up with the loggers and teach them to leave the highlands alone. Westerly of Mount Si, in the clement clime of the low-elevation Tokul Plateau, the forests have been clearcut—*twice*—in the Great Big Western Tree Farm, and a third crop will be chainsaw-size early in the coming century. The predecessor of this guidebook, *Footsore 2,* spent pages on routes in the Tree Mine (big views) and Tree Farm (moody, very moody). This book says goodbye to all that. The roads that put the walking in reasonable day-trip reach are private and gated, and gate policy changes unpredictably and cannot be trusted. Hikers who habitually drive through open gates learn to carry camping gear in the car, prepared for a night inside a locked gate. (However, planned camping is banned and *any* camping may be prosecuted as criminal trespass.) Finally, the "trustworthy" period for legal entry through the gates is weekends-only from the opening of lowland lakes fishing season to the close of the general hunting season, which means that when roads are open to a pedestrian they are swarming with motorized vehicles and weapons loosing lethal missiles. The views and moods remain as always for the adventure-walker but will not be described here.

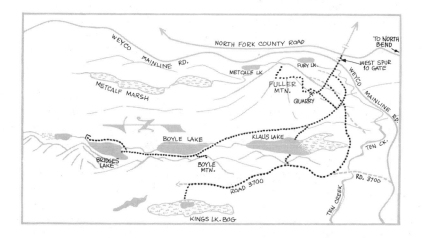

Outside the Mount Si NRCA lies a portion of the GBWTF where gates are the peacelover's friend, barring motorized vehicles during the fall-to-spring months which are ideal for walking the Tokul Plateau.

Go off I-90 on Exit 31 into North Bend. Turn east on North Bend Way 2 blocks and turn north on Ballarat Avenue. Follow this thoroughfare through many changes in name/number until it throws off disguises and reveals itself to be North Fork County Road. At 3.8 miles from North Bend Way is a Y where the right fork is Ernie's Grove Road; take the left (chuckholes, washboard, ruts, shooting galleries) another 3.8 miles to the intersection with Weyerhaeuser's famous (but no longer signed because that would just encourage people) Spur 10, vehicle entry (when the gates are open) to the GBWTM on the right, the GBWTF on the left. Turn left 0.1 mile to West Spur 10 Gate and park (outside), elevation 1003 feet.

Fuller Mountain

Round trip 2½ miles, allow 3 hours
High point 1850 feet, elevation gain 850 feet
All year

A footstool peak isolated from the Cascade front, the Fuller Mountain haystack towers (well, that's going a bit strong) nearly 1000 feet above the Tokul Plateau, prominent from miles away in all directions and commanding a view of surrounding forests and lakes. But first you got to get up it. If you can.

This surveyor first climbed Fuller in 1942, a mere four decades after Frederick Weyerhaeuser, having clearcut the Great Lakes region to the last bush, founded a new empire in the Pacific Northwest by purchasing from his St. Paul neighbor, railroad tsar Jim Hill, thousands of acres of the Northern Pacific Land Grant, paying $6 an acre. Until just 2 years before that first visit by this surveyor, the U.S. Forest Service hoped to gain control of the mountain (and hundreds of thousands of other acres) through revestment (return to the public) of the land grant on the grounds of illegal actions by the grantee and assignees. But the U.S. Supreme Court voted 4–4, one justice abstaining, and the land grant stood, just barely.

The Fuller country had been recently clearcut for the first time when the surveyor arrived. He and his companion, a fellow teenage geology student wondering what the mountain was made of, beat brush from logging roads to Ten Creek, waded its swampy run, beat more brush to the base of the peak, and scrambled the gully rockslide on the northeast edge of the peak. The surveyor's next several ascents were by the same route, which is given prominence here because after five more decades of private propertyship it may once again be the best way to go. If daunted by the following route description, aim for the rockslide. You may not like it but you can't miss it.

Walk by the gate and straight across the Mainline. A few feet north of the large Weyerhaeuser sign, find a boot-beaten track through a 1985 clearcut. In woods at the far edge flows Ten Creek, crossed on a log placed by forestry students from Green River College. You may not wish to try the log if the original handrail has not been replaced, posing the risk of toppling headfirst into the beaver pond. Downstream several hundred steps is the old crossing, as good-bad as ever; half-submerged logs supplemented by a bit of planking permit a non-perilous semi-wade; the creek may be over the boots but rarely to the knees.

Fuller Mountain from beaver pond on Ten Creek. Trail ascends left side of mountain; the old scramble route ascends gully to right skyline

A path ascends to a logging road. A few steps to the left a trail of sorts through the 1984 clearcut is a shortcut to a second logging road. Now, troubles.

In 1975 the Green River students fulfilled a class requirement by building a splendid summit trail. Not a boulevard! Engineered to exclude wheels, many small obstacles of roots and rocks were left intact. Ascending across steep west slopes of the mountain in fine mixed forest, the way attained the north ridge at about 1600 feet and turned south to the summit through dense woods. However, there were views. First, partway up the mountain, on a rockslide was a look down to Klaus Lake. Second, on the ridge the trailbuilders cut a window in the forest, opening out north on Boyle and Bridges Lakes, Metcalf Marsh, various bumps and vales, and the North Fork and Tolt valleys and east to the Cascade front. Third, they cut another window opening west over Klaus Lake and the Tokul Plateau to the Issaquah Alps, downtown Seattle, and the Olympics. The climax vista was just before the final rise to the summit; a short walk left and through woods, following orange dots on trees, led to a mossy bald, a flower glory in spring and in all seasons offering a stunning panorama of the Cascade front from Lake Hancock to Si to North Bend. That was the way it *was*.

The surveyor was pleased to witness the concord between private industry and the public. His senior patrol leader from Troop 324, Howard Millan, had become Weyerhaeuser's first university-trained forester and insisted through the years that he could manage multiple-use just as intelligently as the Forest Service. It was he who gave Pat Cummins—one-time climbing companion of this surveyor and long-time Weyerhaeuser forester-become-professor of forestry at Green River College—authority to build Fuller Trail and Bill Longwell authority to build Tiger Mountain Trail. Millan, himself, built the trail up Mount Philip on the White River and several self-guiding nature trails. He yearned to rehabilitate and preserve the historic Swinging Bridge over the North Fork Snoqualmie as the trailhead from which to rebuild the logging-destroyed trail up Black Creek to Lake Hancock, a route known and loved by generations of Boy Scouts. The surveyor, as journalist, was conducted on tour by the company's Designated Sweet-Talker, who applauded the notion of Millan-style trails. As guidebook writer, the surveyor was led by foresters on a Green River enterprise done on contract with the company, the High Yield Forest Trail.

However, things seemed to be afoot (wrong word!) in the bottom-line-calculating gray matter at company headquarters. Hikers began to feel Somebody Up There didn't like them. The Fuller country, whose peak and lakes had been for several decades and more the area's favorite lowland pedestrian destination, entered a time of troubles.

Returning for a new edition of *Footsore 2,* the surveyor found the start of the summit trail obliterated by the 1984 clearcut. (Elsewhere, he could find no trace of the company's pride, the High Yield Forest Trail!) Walking "second logging road" (see above), a bit to the left, he intersected the "first logging road," turned right on it, and shortly spotted a mass of flags at the top of the clearcut and followed a rude path up the slash to intersect the trail. (He scouted back along the trail, over many down logs, to the original trailhead at a small quarry, the trail attained from below by turning right on "second road" and then left on the quarry road.) Volunteers are reported to have reopened this original beginning. Many hikers have reported they couldn't find the trail no how, no where.

More clearcuts. More confusion of logging roads. And the denouement, METRO SLUDGE. Sludge-sprayed seedlings grow faster. But the stuff stinks something terrible for a while and the landscape looks like Nuclear Winter. Signs warn that breathing the air may be a hazard to your health. Hikers who forge through the new clearcut slash and dare the black landscape report the Green River College trail has many many blowdowns and very few bootprints.

In a locale that in public ownership would long since have been a state park thronged every weekend of the year, hikers feel unwelcome. Howie never did get permission to rebuild the Lake Hancock trail. His nature trails have vanished. His Mount Philip trail survives only through nurturing by loving boots.

If determined to climb Fuller, consider the alternative of the rockslide gully. Returned home, watch the TV commercials and wonder why some of the money spent on this attempt to win the hearts and minds of the populace is not spent perpetuating the memory of Weyerhaeuser Forester No. 1, Howard Millan.

Kings Lake Bog

Round trip 5 miles, allow 3 hours
High point 1003 feet, minor elevation gain
All year

Though a spot of open water has been given the name of "lake," the bog is the attraction, ⅔ mile long and ¼ mile wide, the biggest and best sphagnum bog of the region. Come in late spring when the entire bog is a pink sea of kalmia in bloom, in summer to sniff the aromatic Labrador tea and watch the meat-eating sundew have lunch, and in fall to pick a hatful of wild cranberries.

Kings Lake Bog

From West Spur 10 Gate, walk to the "first logging road" (see "Fuller Mountain") and turn left to the four-way intersection at the foot of Fuller Mountain. Continue straight ahead a scant 1 mile, then right 1 long mile on road 3700. Find the location of the bog by the tall cedar snags (drowned by beaver floods) above the screen of trees bordering the shore. Pick a short but probably mean route through the slash of the 1985 clearcut; look for fisherman footprints.

Klaus, Boyle, and Bridges Lakes

Round trip 6½ miles, allow 4 hours
High point 1034 feet, elevation gain 200 feet
All year

Less than a decade ago, the surveyor could say, and did, "The somber lakes curving in a chain around the foot of Fuller Mountain make a fine walk in themselves or combine with the peak to fill out a day. The half-lake, half-marsh openings in second-growth forest ... offer splendid birdwatching." The way we were....

Boyle Lake and Fuller Mountain

At the four-way intersection at the foot of Fuller Mountain, a sidetrip leads to the shore of Klaus Lake. Go left about 200 feet, then right a scant ¼ mile on a gravel road and then a jeep track, and finally on a footpath to the shore of Klaus Lake, 983 feet, a long mile from Spur 10 gate. Gaze through reeds and grasses and quiet waters, watch ducks swim, and perhaps hear a loon call.

Back at the four-way junction, go north on the road that passes to the left of Fuller Mountain. In the next ½ mile are three short spurs, each with views down to Klaus Lake. The first has a path, of sorts, to the shore. It was here the trustworthy photographer watched a pair of curious beavers watching the curious photographer. It would have make a great telephoto picture but the trustworthy photographer did not have a telephoto lens with him. Look for recent beaver logging operations along the lakeshore.

Beyond the Klaus spur the logging road splits. Take the right, straight ahead, bending left to follow the outlet creek of Boyle Lake. The road swerves away right, leaving the last few hundred feet of old railroad grade-become-trail untouched—not by company benevolence but by decree of the State Wildlife Department. At a scant 1 mile from the Klaus Lake junction is the outlet of Boyle Lake, 1034 feet.

What used to be the surveyor's favorite walk in the Fuller country used to begin here, the enchanting 1¼ miles of the "Great Lakeshore & Northern Railroad." The open, parklike grade closely followed Boyle Lake, many a path out from big second-growth cedars and firs to spots for watching birds and gaping at the loftiness of Fuller Mountain. Beyond the lake-end marsh was the lovely little inlet creek, at one point beaver-dammed to a marshy pond. From this, the outlet of Bridges Lake, the rail grade continued by more reeds and birds, petering out in marshes at the end of the lake.

In 1993 the surveyor's field agent checked in. Clearcutting had pretty well finished shipping the Fuller forests overseas. Though the Wildlife Department restrictions held the loggers at the legal distance from the shore of Boyle Lake, windthrow so blockaded the trail that it no longer could be considered a walk; a hungry fisherman might think it a worthwhile crawl. The agent gave up in disgust and therefore couldn't report whether Bridges Lake, too, has been lost to the iron dictate of the accountant's bottom line.

Sunday Creek and Lake
(Map—page 93)

Round trip to footlog 8 miles, allow 5 hours
High point 2000 feet, elevation gain 500 feet
April–November

Spend too much time in the GBWTF and GBWTM and this hike will shock you out of your socks. (A good idea—see below.) Not the lake, which is nice enough, but in a land of hundreds of lakes has to be ranked run-of-the-mill. Nor even the creek, which is a jim-dandy, but so are myriad others hereabouts. No, it's not the water. It's the trees. Accustomed as a hiker is in this area to tree-farm trees, cute little seedlings, vigorous Christmas trees, and second-growth that's half-a-century old, the sudden confrontation with ancient forest is enough to drop you to your knees. What explains this miracle of preservation? How did such forest survive at such low elevation? Someplace in the past of the U.S. Forest Service there's an unsung hero, someone who fought to keep this valley with its trees on while those all around were losing theirs. And now the Alpine Lakes Wilderness has assumed the heritage. So when weary of panoramas from clearcuts, come here.

Drive North Fork County Road 8.7 miles beyond Spur 10 (see "Fuller Country") to the plank bridge across Sunday Creek at 16.3 miles from North Bend Way. Continue 1.1 miles to an unsigned sideroad right, newly but eternally gated shut. Park where you can without blocking the road, carefully, elevation 1500 feet.

Moraines dumped by the monster glacier from Canada dammed all the valleys of the Cascade front hereabouts. Still remaining are Lakes Hancock and Calligan. But the largest lake was that of the North Fork Snoqualmie, 6 miles long and a mile and more wide, occupying both the North Fork valley and that of a major tributary, Sunday Creek. Deltas pretty well filled the lake. Since then the river and creek have meandered over the former lakebed; presently they run on opposite sides of the valley much of the way, Sunday Creek over a wide avenue of gravel bars. On a hot Sunday the valley rings with laughter of little children in the area's favorite water playground. Contemplative adults find peace and birds in meander-cutoff sloughs, oxbow lakes, and marshes. Lying below 1600 feet, the lakebed is open for walking when ridges above are gleaming white.

For more than half the length of the old lake, Sunday Creek maintains its independence. At the crossing by the North Fork road the gravel bars and sandbars and pools (skipping stones, building castles, wading) are thronged every sunny Sunday. The grown-up who feels self-conscious wading in public is tantalized on a hot day of late summer, when the creek is low yet icy, by the thought of assuming a costume of shorts and sneakers for a wet walk up the middle of the creek, doing a round trip of 6 miles or until the toes drop off.

Walk the road-trail 0.7 mile from the gate to a Y and go right. In 0.3 mile more, where the main road curves right to cross Sunday Creek

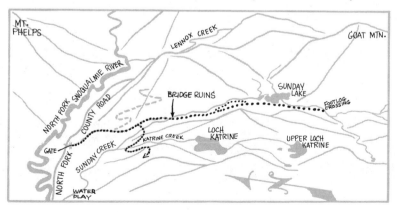

Sunday Lake

(but doesn't, the bridge for the ascent to Loch Katrine is gone, the better to blue your knees), follow a ruder road straight ahead, left, 0.4 mile to where another bridge is gone. Ford or seek a footlog, upstream or down, elevation 1650 feet.

The trail sets out on a narrow roadway, the first portion a logging track of the 1960s, the rest of the way to the lake a relic of ancient mining idiocy. In 1 long mile the road-trail passes campsites and sidepaths to the lake. But there's a better way. Several hundred feet from the former trailhead, spot an old logging road going obscurely left. In a short bit, at the end of the logging, the start of virgin forest, it yields to genuine trail, none other than the ancient and honorable Sunday Creek trail. This is The Trip—a wilderness arboretum of mossy logs, fern-hung hillsides, cool-shadowy sitting spots beside the brawl and splash of Sunday Creek, and wonderfully "decadent" old forest of fir, hemlock, cedar, hardwoods, and snags, a very different experience from a monotonous monocultural Douglas fir plantation of young, thrifty trees that never will achieve middle age. Near the lake the trail rejoins the road.

The lake is worth a look, but since trees are the stars here continue on. The trail goes up and down, rougher and skinnier, about ½ mile along the lakeshore. In another ½ mile it drops off the sidehill to cross the creek at 2000 feet and proceed onward, upward into the Alpine Lakes Wilderness. But the footlog crossing is perhaps far enough.

Moon Valley
(Map—page 96)

The freeway millions gape at the huge leap of Mount Si from the North Bend Plain. A few approach close, bend necks back and back, get a crick while eye-climbing the cliffs, looking for mountain goats. Some want still more. They risk chunks of falling mountain squishing them in their beds, a crazed river washing their furniture to Puget Sound, a forest fire carbonizing their eyebrows.

Ernie's Grove began as a campground and picnic park during the era when it lay at the extreme limit for a comfortable weekend drive from Seattle in tin lizzie or merry Oldsmobile. City folks could drive through the log arch, pay two-bits per car, and unload the picnic basket or erect the wall tent. For a few bits more they could rent a cabin from Ernie Hodgeon, and spend the summer. In time the vacation retreat was transformed to exurbia, accompanied across the river by the

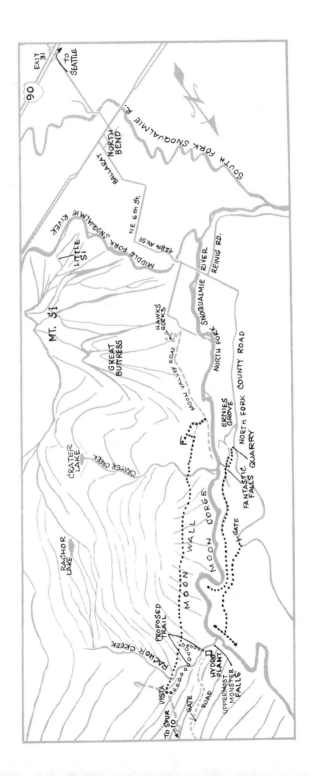

community of Moon Valley. So fully and lovingly was the scene privatized that nowadays the public can't get close enough to the river to hit it with a rock.

Moon Valley is named for the star child who was kidnapped by sea-beings, escaped, and swam up the river to settle here, having in the course of the myth been transformed into none other a personage than the Moon, later renamed Si. Above Moon Valley rises the Moon Wall. Running through it is the river, exiting from the Moon Gorge.

The Moon Gorge (Black Canyon)

Downstream from its confluence with Black Creek, where until the 1980s the Swinging Bridge crossed to where used to be the Lake Hancock trail, the North Fork continues a while babbling through a tree farm. A very few minutes later, the same water will be meandering through cow farms. But first it has a last wild fling, dropping a tumultuous 400 feet into a gorge, gaining power from all-waterfall Rachor Creek, cutting the foot of the Moon Wall the full length of the 2-mile (as the river runs) canyon.

Only kayakers know the Black Canyon intimately, the dozen-odd cataracts, two of them monsters, which as of this writing never have been run, the Last Great Challenges of the region. Will river-runners continue to have a try? The Friends of the Snoqualmie Rivers, backed by the Northwest Rivers Council, are resisting Pacific Hydro, the "small hydro" entrepreneurship whose McLeod Ridge Project would divert the publicly owned river from the cataracts into a pipe to make kilowatts.

As of 1994 there is no (zero, zilch) guaranteed way for the public to so much as see a work of Nature that would attract masses of admiring eyes—if it could be seen.

Once upon a time the surveyor followed a route pioneered by deranged fishermen and gained a view of the uppermost of the monster cataracts (see out-of-print *Footsore 2*). Coming to this edition, he sought counsel from kayaker Jim Good, who described a way to the lowermost monster cataract. Since the photographer was going to have to go there anyhow, the surveyor assigned him to spend an easy afternoon scouting the route. At the conclusion of 3 scrambling days, the photographer and Mrs. Photographer reported they had surveyed the entire canyon. Their judgment: "Be warned, readers, the fearless surveyor cannot be trusted. Getting a picture of Fantastic Falls is a nightmare. However, there is much to see in Moon Gorge that is easy and rewarding. The views are best in winter, the trees bare of leaves. All in all, the three days were worth the effort."

Fantastic Falls (Lowermost Monster)

Round trip 3 to 4 miles, allow 3 hours
High point 620 feet, elevation gain negligible
All year

Drive North Fork County Road (see "Fuller Country") 0.4 mile past Ernie's Grove Road to a small gravel pit barred by a yellow gate. Park here (space for a couple-three cars), elevation 620 feet.

Walk into the pit and follow the single track of an abandoned road to the right, contouring a steep bank. In a few feet look down to houses of Ernie's Grove. Paved with soft moss and shaded by maples and firs, the old road turns upstream, gently undulating, the river only occasionally glimpsed but ever heard. In a scant 1 mile, the way intersects the pipeline road (also a single-track trail) from Ernie's Grove (from private property there, no public access).

The rumble of Fantastic Falls almost literally shakes you in your boots. For a glimpse, walk the pipeline road-trail downstream a few feet and spot the surveyor's (actually, Jim Good's) "easy way to the river," an extremely steep path, featuring a 5-foot near-vertical rock step, slippery when wet. This definitely is not for the young or the decrepit or, in the photographer's opinion, for anybody in-between. Best leave it to the breed that enjoys placing mortal flesh in fragile plastic craft and flinging it into cataracts. Actually, the only view of the falls is halfway down; at the riverbank the monster is out of sight. Be content to listen from the pipeline.

But don't give up the trip. Walk downstream on the trail, blasted from cliffs, a scant ½ mile to spectacular views into the gorge. When the path starts steeply downhill, turn around and walk back upstream, passing the kayakers' "easy trail" on smooth tread, a few little looks to the river. At about ¾ mile from "easy trail," the tread narrows, crosses the steep, loose gravel of Suicide Slide [see "Rachor Falls (Uppermost Monster)"] and reenters woods.

Pass the waterworks of the City of Snoqualmie. (Do not meddle; if the city's water seems imperiled, presence anywhere on this entire route probably will make you subject to arrest.) There being no road to the site, helicopters must have brought in the construction machinery. In a scant ¼ mile more the trail abruptly ends at a cliff. Metal pipes sticking out of the ground and some old wire-wrapped wooden pipes are the only indications that the trail overlays a pipeline. Poke around the scene a bit. Pretty little waterfalls. Access paths to the river, not easy but feasible for nimble feet.

Rachor Falls (Uppermost Monster)

Round trip 4 miles, allow 3 hours
High point 1050 feet, elevation gain 50 feet
All year

Drive North Fork Road 1.4 miles past Ernie's Grove junction. Spot a triangular parking area and a gated road to the right. Park here, elevation 1000 feet.

The preceding gorge trip to the Lowermost Monster may be closed to hikers by the City of Snoqualmie; this one may be shut off by World War III. A sign announces that King County plans a public shooting facility. A square mile of Weyerhaeuser's Northern Pacific Land Grant

Rachor Falls and North Fork Snoqualmie River

inheritance would be leased, not bought. Processing for the gun range would cut through years of normal urbanization-permitting procedures. Upon expiration of the lease, exactly when the sprawl of Puget Sound City had made dense development economic this far east, Weyerhaeuser could proceed instantly, unimpeded by red tape, to building another in its series of New Cities.

During the term of the lease, North Bend and Snoqualmie would find themselves the most heavily armed communities outside Big City Saturday Night. Gunners would be drawn from a dozen counties. Planners are receiving requests for every manner of missile-loosing device from slingshots to (well, not quite) the ICBM. Walkers come for the peace and quiet of the Moon Wall and the Mount Si NRCA would recuperate by going to the Kingdome for a heavy metal rock show riot.

Walk the gated road about ½ mile, where the gorge brink is close to the right. Look 4000 feet up the Moon Wall. Look down the gravel chute of Suicide Slide 400 feet to the river. Even should Snoqualmie close the pipeline trail, you will not wish to descend the slide unless you are a trout fisherman missing a full set of flies.

Continue on the road ¼ mile and turn right. At the next junction stay right (straight ahead) and descend a bit to a T. For a view of the Uppermost Monster and Rachor Creek, turn right to the road-end; a slot in the trees opens a skinny vignette of the famous scene. Be satisfied. There's no easy way to get there. Walk to the other end of the T for a view upriver.

The photographer spotted on the east side of the river about 500 feet upstream from Rachor Creek a new-looking road and some sort of structure. If Pacific Hydro has not yet got the North Fork in a pipe, Rachor Creek has not been so lucky (see "The Moon Wall").

The Moon Wall

Round trip 5 miles, allow 4 hours
High point 2000 feet, elevation gain 1600 feet
All year

In the decade before World War II, an argonaut found a pot of gold or something in the headwaters of Rachor Creek. Weyerhaeuser not having yet bulled a logging road from the North Fork, he scratched a track from Moon Valley across the precipice. After he went away to war or something, a gypo logger chanced by, bought cutting rights from Weyerhaeuser, and high-graded the forest of the wall, hauling out a few of the fattest trees on what the 1960 USGS Mount Si quadrangle calls "Jeep Trail." The DNR used the route for two timber sales, the first soon after World War II, the last in the 1970s. The clearcuts extended to the boundary of state land. Weyerhaeuser did not finish the clearing for two self-evident reasons: (1) harvesting of the cliffy wall would have cost a lot and (2) the preservation of Mount Si had become such a lively public issue that the superb ancient forest so lightly touched by the gypos had less value as logs than as trade goods. And lo, the Grand Exchange saved a trail that was to become one of the supreme glories of the Mount Si NRCA.

A problem: The DNR failed to acquire permanent easement across a sliver of private land on the jeep "trail." Another problem: When accelerated home-building loomed in Moon Valley, the DNR failed to acquire that sliver. Houses got built. What's now to be done? Either easement must be purchased or adverse possession pursued on the basis of a half-century of unobstructed public use. Until then, hikers must detour.

Drive North Fork County Road (see "Fuller Country") exactly 2 miles from North Bend Way, turn right on SE 92, which twists and turns through different numbers to become at last Moon Valley Road. At 1.55 miles from North Fork Road, a rude road climbs steeply right. It has the look of being private but is not, though it serves as driveway to a pair of new houses. It is in fact the start—on DNR land—of the jeep "trail." A person can legally beat brush above the private property to return to public land. To do so, park on Moon Valley Road, out of the dogs' sight, elevation 450 feet.

A few steps up from Moon Valley Road on the driveway, still on state land, note to the right an old road diminished to a trail, halfheartedly blocked by a feeble fence. Ascend this right fork 820 feet from Moon Valley Road. Turn left, off the road-trail, due north (by compass) exactly 254 feet to pass the private 5.28 acres and two houses. Angle down to the jeep road beyond an old gravel pit signed "private" but actually on state land. (The residents cannot be blamed for overstepping their legal rights. Upon moving into new houses they discovered they had invaded the freedom country of the night-riding joy boys and the Sunday-afternoon beer-can blasters.) As of 1994 this detour is a quarter-hour bushwhack on public land. Volunteers are urged to whack out a tread and the DNR to install an official public trailhead sign.

The jeep "trail" ascends past the gravel pit to a flat, 950 feet, beneath imposing cliffs. See the Great Buttress, the white thread of waterfalling Rachor Creek, Fuller Mountain, and the Tokul Plateau. The bouldery, brawling cataracts of Crater Creek, 1040 feet, will be (once the way is made family-easy) a famous place to get out the sardine sandwiches and root beer and turn the kids loose to wade. Just beyond is the rotting jackstraw of a small clearcut, quickly squirmed through to a resumption of jeep "trail."

At precisely this point the "Weyerhaeuser preserve" (now public) begins. The hiker assumes the forest is virgin until he/she notes very occasional stumps cut by double-bitted axes and misery whips and donkey engines of pretty long ago. On his first exploration the surveyor followed very fresh cougar tracks through brand-new snow; never quite caught up; wasn't sure he wanted to. On his latest he found the path well beaten but, as indicated by logs fallen across the way, mainly by walkers no taller than 2 to 3 feet and innocent of shoes.

The old road hasn't seen a wheel in decades but is easy walking in deep forest, though it becomes somewhat less easy every bad winter. In many spots the grade is slumping away. The blowout channels of creeks are getting broader and deeper; the hiker here in deep forest cannot understand why, unable as he/she is to see or guess the flood-gushing clearcuts high above. The way goes by big boulders that have fallen from the cliffs over the centuries, including some that fell in 1984, bashing down big trees, and through groves of alder-maple, mixed forest, all-conifer forest of fir, hemlock, and cedar up to 3 feet and more in diameter. The bouldery fan of Wowfow Creek is passed and two blowout fans of the 1980s. The ear harkens to an awesome roar—Moon River, directly below in Black Canyon. Abruptly the firs are 5 feet in diameter, ancient beauties, mingled with even larger snags, bird condos. Another roar is heard—Rachor Creek, white water the full length of its canyon from hanging valley to the river cauldron.

The jeep "trail" swings into Rachor canyon, jungled up by alders that can be penetrated to a safe ford, leading to a short scramble up moraine gravel to the modern logging road. Why bother? The ancient grove at 2½ miles, 2000 feet, is the proper turnaround.

More might be done on the Moon Wall without intruding on wildlife refuges. Two suggestions follow.

Footsore 2 (out of print) describes the walk to Rachor Vista as follows: Drive North Fork County Road to Spur 10 (see "Fuller Country"). In season and on the days the gates are open to public vehicles (again, see "Fuller Country"), drive through East Spur 10 Gate, elevation 1000 feet. Otherwise walk. In 1 long mile cross the North Fork Snoqualmie

Rachor Falls at end of Moon Wall jeep trail; this is what causes the big racket you hear (but never see) while hiking the trail

and turn right on road 4200. In 1¼ miles from the river, the excitement begins as the road tilts steeply up to climb the northerly continuation of the Moon Wall, the front scarp of the Cascades. Three creeks are crossed, each such a tumble in springtime as to be more air than water, delicious spots to eat an apple and a can of kipper snacks. The view grows step by step, climaxing on a promontory, 2200 feet, 4 miles from East Spur 10 Gate; the panorama is down to the North Fork in its Moon Gorge, west to Fuller Mountain, the Issaquah Alps, Seattle, and the Olympics, and north to Mount Sultan and the San Juan Islands.

This Rachor Vista, a great walk when the gates are closed, can be a shortcut to the ancient forest of the Moon Wall. That old miners' "Jeep Trail" crossed Rachor Creek near here, and just below the promontory can be found an old spur road that leads to Rachor Creek. Cross on a handy log and scramble uphill in the ancient trees to the jeep "trail." That's one way to do it. The surveyor's route crossed the creek exactly at the end of the jeep "trail," as already noted. But construction of a new trail from Rachor Vista could be a link in a loop walk, which would spend twice the time in glorious ancience.

The other suggestion will take exploratory effort. At a point on road 4200 before it strikes steeply up into the hanging valley of Rachor Creek, a gated road goes off right to the "small hydro" installation close to Rachor Creek and not far above the North Fork. The lowest of the Rachor Creek cataracts might be a good destination for a hike in itself; possibly this is the closest pedestrian view of the Uppermost Monster cataract of the North Fork. Elevation, about 1000 feet. Distance from Spur 10 Gate, about 3 miles. Pioneers might locate a safe, interesting, and ecologically sensitive trail route up to the (projected) Moon Wall Loop. Watch this space in the next edition.

Little Si
(Map—page 105)

Round trip from bridge 5 miles, allow 3 hours
High point 1576 feet, elevation gain 1200 feet
All year

Mount Si's footstool peaklet is as old as the Canadian glacier that rode over and around it, smoothing and pucking, as old as the seismic shakings that thrust up the Moon Wall and this lesser byblow, and for a century (or millennia?) people have been scrambling to the summit to gaze out upon the North Bend Plain.

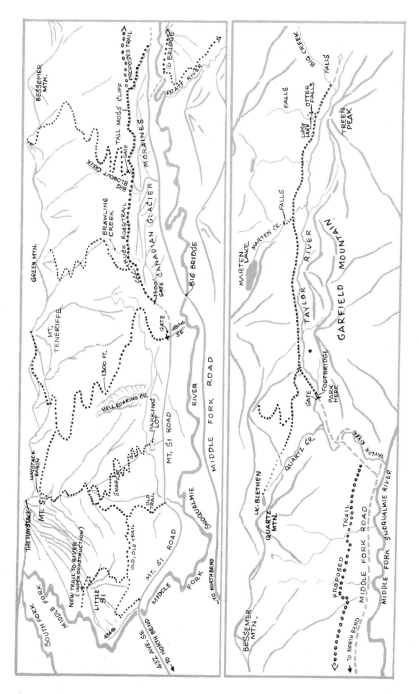

105

Thursday Hikers club on top of Little Si

However, until 1985 there never was a real trail, only the boot-scrubbed rocks of the scrambling route. Then your surveyor decided the peak was needed in a new edition to publicize the wanted extension of the Mount Si Conservation Area. He asked Will Thompson, a Hard-Core Ptarmigan famed for explorations in the North Cascades in the 1930s, to take a look. Will looked—and flagged—and built ¾ mile of new trail to the summit. In October he led "Thompson's Army," from the Issaquah Alps Trails Club and The Mountaineers, on a general cleanup and improvement of the previously existing mile of boot-beaten path. The group assembled on top to hoist the flag and sing the anthem, celebrating the inauguration of what since has become the most popular summit hike in the area, combining the spooky green cleft between Big Si and Little Si, beneath the Great Overhang, and the summit views—all on a hike easily done in a lazy afternoon and open to walking the year-round.

Go off I-90 on Exit 31 into North Bend and drive east on North Bend Way, old U.S. 10. From the split continue on the left half (North Bend Way) 0.8 mile and turn left on Mt. Si Road 0.3 mile to the Middle Fork bridge. Across the bridge immediately turn left on 434 Avenue and immediately left again to the parking area, elevation 500 feet. (If the parking area is full, as always on weekends, do not seek space on 434th; it's full-up with homes. Retreat to North Bend Way, lots of shoulder space for parking and only 0.3 mile extra walking, which couldn't kill you.)

Walk ¼ mile on 434th to the signed trail. Ascend steeply ⅓ mile to just beyond an old Y where the road levels out and makes a sweeping turn left; here, at another Y, the Old Old Big Si Trail goes off right. Follow the left-sweeping fork to its end at a creek, 700 feet, in ¼ mile—¾ mile from the bridge.

The trail leaves the mixed forest grown up since a 1960s logging show and enters virgin forest grown up since the fires that swept most of Little and Big Si in the nineteenth century. The trees are not big but none are "farmed." This is the look of a *young* virgin forest. In ¼ mile the trail rounds a swamp bowl of old beaver ponds, 840 feet. The scramble route climbs left to the rockslide that leads to the gullies, where in olden days the Climbing Course of The Mountaineers annually sent mobs of novices upward to their fates. (A prominent buttress in the middle of the gully system used to bear the spray-paint lettering "Manning's Perch," because that's where the surveyor, when Climbing Chairman, was wont to position himself to scream at stupid novices and idiot instructors.)

Keep right, ascending into the rift where the little fault block split off from the big one and the glacier squeezed through. The ice seems scarcely to have melted, so chilly it is here, where the sun so rarely shines. Giant boulders tumbled from above are strewn through the dark forest and under the boulders are trogs, and if on a winter day a hiker peers down to the interiors he/she may see troglodytes peering back. One becomes aware of the cliff close left—and then of a cliff *overhead!* It is the Great Overhang, often admired from I-90 but shocking to be discovered hanging heavy heavy over thy head!

The path tops out at an 1100-foot saddle and descends a haunting glen of old hemlocks and mossy splinters of fault scarp. At 1000 feet, ¾ mile from the beaver pond, begins the ¾ mile of Will's (1985) Trail. Setting out up a fissure that geologist Will diagnoses as probably dating from a great quake of about 200 years ago, the way alternates between steep leaps and gentlings, climbing the north ridge of Little Si from small but tall Douglas firs to spindly fir. Windows open out this way and that. One investigates a brink to the left—and shrinks back from the straight-down view to the bottom of the rift. Soon beyond, the way emerges on the summit, 1576 feet.

The mossy balds have grown very little vegetation since the times of ice and fire, mainly shrubby lodgepole pine, copses of manzanita, sprawls of kinnikinnick, clumps of serviceberry and ocean spray, and a glory of May blossoms. The views are up up up the Si scarp to the Haystack, north to the Great Buttress, and beyond to Fuller Mountain; from McClellan Butte and Mailbox/Garcia and Grouse and Washington to the long stretch of Rattlesnake and out to Tiger and Cougar and Grand and the Olympics. But the main show is down, to the Pleistocene lakebed and the towns of Snoqualmie and North Bend, old U.S. 10 and older Sunset Highway and new I-90, the thriving river, dilapidating Weyerhaeuser mill, the cows.

The Snoqualmie Valley Trails Club has battled brush down a rough route from the Little Si trail to the river. A finished trail could add a riverbank picnic to the day's pleasures. In any event, the enormous popularity of the new Little Si trail (and all the old Big Si trails) indicates a need for loop trails to spread the boots around. A survey of plant and animal habitats should be made and then a plan developed for new loop trails, pleasurable and non-destructive.

Mount Si
(Map—page 105)

Round trip 2, 3½, 8 miles, allow 2, 4, 8 hours
High point 1600, 2100, 3900 feet, elevation gain 850, 1350, 3200 feet
All year (partway)

In 1964 Tom Miller presented to the Literary Fund Committee of The Mountaineers a plan for a guidebook. The plan was adopted by the committee, he proceeded with the implementation, and more than any other person or combination of persons he was responsible for *100 Hikes in Western Washington,* published in 1966. The book invented a new style in hiking-guide format and set a pattern for guidebooks as environmental tools parallel to Dave Brower's historic Exhibit Format volumes, begun with 1960's *This Is the American Earth.* That fame

At 3.5 miles, the Mount Si trail reaches the summit ridge of Mount Si.

was not Miller's aim is proven by his eagerness to let others take the credit. His motivation, as he explained to the committee, was that his career was suffering because come sunny spring he couldn't get any work done. From all over the company, a parade marched through his office, everybody wanting directions on how to climb Si. And so The Mountaineers got into the guidebook business.

Almost since this majestic hunk was named for an 1862 settler, Josiah Merritt ("Uncle Si"), it has drawn hikers. After being for generations the best-known (well, perhaps second to Rainier) and most-climbed (by some 50,000 a year) mountain in the state, it received overdue recognition as the superstar of a Natural Resources Conservation Area, flagship for a wildly exciting new concept in management of state lands.

Drive Mt. Si Road (see "Little Si") 2 miles from the Snoqualmie River bridge to the enormous trailhead parking lot, elevation 750 feet.

From the low-valley lushness of hardwood-conifer forest, the trail ascends the steep valley wall and enters a nineteenth century burn featuring a new forest of firs up to 2 feet thick, plus large black snags of the old forest. In 1 long mile, at 1600 feet, a rock slab-cliff (a glacier job) gives a window out to the valley floor, to I-90, to the moraine of the Canadian glacier sweeping in an arc from the Middle Fork valley over the South Fork to the Cedar River.

In ¾ mile more, at 2100 feet, the way levels at Snag Flat's grove of Douglas firs; though fire-blackened, they were big enough to survive the conflagrations that denuded most of Si in the nineteenth century and remote enough to escape the loggers. However, they at last are succumbing, weakened by the fire, and most are snagtops. Here in the

A nurse log in the octopuslike grip of a hemlock tree, about a mile up the Mount Si trail

ancient-forest gloom, beside the lovely creek, is a pleasant spot for picnicking, a satisfying winter–early spring turnaround.

Usually in March or April (often earlier), the snow melts on the
higher slopes. The trail can then be climbed 2⅓ more miles to Haystack Basin, 3900 feet, 4 miles. Clamber around the boulders under
the wall of the Haystack, 4167-foot final peak of Si. But don't climb it
unless you know what you're doing on rock—and even if you do, don't
climb it when other people are around; there is danger of being hit by
falling bodies.

From the edge of the fault scarp plunging more than 3000 feet to
the valley, admire the green pastures, the geometry of streets in North
Bend and Snoqualmie, the bugs scurrying along I-90, and the panorama from Rainier to Rattlesnake to the Issaquah Alps to towers of
downtown Seattle to the Olympics.

The preceding route description is the New Si Trail built in the
1960s by the DNR (aided by volunteer Mountaineers and others) to re-
place the Old Si Trail, which had been blotched by a clearcut of private
lands.

The Old Si Trail actually is as good as ever and gets its own tender
loving care by a crew of volunteer maintenance workers who like the
route for being lonesomer, at least to the 3000-foot junction with the
New Trail, and shorter by a mile, thanks to a steeper grade. The
trailhead parking area is unsigned but unmistakable at a yellow fire
hydrant on Mt. Si Road 1.5 miles from the Middle Fork bridge.

The Old Old Si Trail was built by North Benders and formally
dedicated on May 10, 1931, by a forty-five-contestant race to the summit; the winning time was 1 hour, 24 minutes. (On a winter day early
in 1948, the surveyor left a coffee shop in North Bend and 1 hour, 20
minutes later arrived at the lip of Haystack Basin. Very strong coffee.)
In the late 1950s the property at the trailhead was developed, instigat-
ing construction of the Old Trail. Starting from what is now 434th, the
Old Old way ascended to an alder-forest flat and campsite by a creek—
none other than the creek at the 700-foot Y of the Little Si trail. There
was a Y then, too, the left to the scramble route up Little Si, the right to
Big Si. Bits of the latter's tread can be found, though most was obliterated by the logging road that instigated the New Trail. This road leads
from the Y to the Old Trail at the clearcut.

The Old Old Old Trail, by which The Mountaineers made the
club's first ascent of a mountain, in 1907, probably went up from the
rift between Little Si and Big Si. Thought is being given to constructing a New New Trail along the route of the Old Old Old.

Mount Teneriffe
(Map—page 105)

Round trip 14 miles, allow 10 hours
High point 4788 feet, elevation gain 4000 feet
May–November

The largest of the Canary Islands is Teneriffe (also spelled with a single *f*). A 12,192-foot volcanic peak on the island is named Mount Teyde, or Teide, and also called the Peak of Tenerife. The surveyor has no idea how the companion of Si got a Canary connection. This titillation aside, the attraction lies in the fact that on a day when the Si trail is bumper to bumper from trailhead to Haystack, Teneriffe may be lonesome. As with Si, a person needn't go to the top for a wealth of views.

Drive Mt. Si Road (see "Mount Si") 1.1 miles past the Si trailhead to School Bus Turnaround. Reverse-turning to the left is a woods road. The gate has been eternally shut to public vehicles since the late 1980s. Park here, elevation 950 feet.

The road-trail sidehills forest and stumps west 2 miles, ascending gradually to 1300 feet. The old map shows the "jeep trail" crossing a nameless intermittent stream. In the mid-1960s a textbook case of illegal (then merely immoral) logging practices destabilized the headwaters. The first in a continuing series of hell-roaring blowouts gouged a boggling canyon and swept down to the Snoqualmie thousands of tons of soil that nevermore will grow forest. The replacement road built to scalp the ridge refrained from crossing Hell-Roaring Nameless Canyon—until just above the spot where loggers triggered the blowout.

At 3200 feet, 2 steep, switchbacking miles from the 1300-foot level, the consciousness expands as the road-trail emerges from virgin forest into the 1960s Georgia-Pacific clearcut, which even in the 1990s catches the eyes (and perhaps opens them wide) of the I-90 traveler. The Horrible Example photos of the foreground have as a background a panorama from Rattlesnake to McClellan Butte, Rainier rising above it all. The I-90 route up the moraine holds a fascination; the morbid ear dwells on the loudness of the roar even this high.

Far enough? If not, continue switchbacking up in new-growing forest which in the NRCA never again will hear the whine of the chainsaw. Avoid a spur left to Si, whose Haystack soon appears, the top occupied by a bunch of human bananas. At about 3700 feet the proper route heads east. The trick here is to attend closely to the map and not climb too high too soon. Do not take spurs toward the ridge crest;

Mailbox Peak from Mount Teneriffe

choose the one and only road-trail that swings around the jut of a prominent spur ridge at 4000 feet to a big-view promontory and, in spring, a big snowbank. Dropping to round the head of a shallow little valley, the way then climbs to a 4200-foot saddle, 2 miles from the 3200-foot viewpoint. Views, now, down to Rachor Lake and the North Fork Snoqualmie.

At last the route leaves road and clearcut, following the rounded crest of the forested summit ridge east on a very faint trail, easy and safe. The surveyor's favorite season for the ascent is late spring, the trail under snow. After ups and downs and a final short, steep up, in 1 mile the trees shrink and vanish. Mossy rocks of the bald summit are brightened by phlox, lupine, and paintbrush. The 4788-foot summit (which in contrast to Si's treacherous Haystack requires no dangerous scrambling) has a view guaranteed to shut your mouth. The plunge to the valley is longer than from Si. And there is Si to look at, ever growing a fresh crop of bananas. And Washington and McClellan Butte and Mailbox/Garcia. And Rattlesnake and other Issaquah Alps. And Green, Garfield, Russian Buttes. And peaks of the Cascade Crest, Glacier, Baker, Rainier, and the North Cascades.

CCC Truck Road Trail
(Map—page 105)

At the turn of the century, a trail for foot and stock ascended the Middle Fork valley to the "gopher holes" of Dutch Miller and his companion swarm of incurable optimists. In the 1920s the "lokie loggers" pushed rails past Taylor River and up the Pratt. In the Great Depression, the industry having picked up its tracks and pulled out of the valley, the Civilian Conservation Corps (CCC) arrived to serve the American responsibility of bringing every province of God's earth under man's gas-powered wheels. Starting from what is now Mt. Si Road, the Three C's bulldozed a truck track up moraines of the Canadian glacier and contoured the valley wall high above the site of the Pleistocene lake, at last descending to join the rail grade near old Camp Brown, just short of the Taylor River.

The conclusion of World War II inaugurated the sport of four-wheeling. Command cars and scout cars, jeeps and peeps, assembled in platoons, companies, and divisions for the fun run from Taylor River to Goldmeyer Hot Springs. On a day in 1949 the surveyor, intending to climb Mount Garfield, drove as far as a rickety railroad trestle, watched a convoy of khaki vehicles loaded with giggling vets rattle the planks, quailed, and turned back. Downvalley from the Taylor, however, in the mid-1950s he and his new young family found a second home on CCC Road, great for bouncing a colicky baby to sleep, for tumbling waterfalls and kiddies' wading pools, and for quarrying chunks of granite for a living-room fireplace. As forests regrew the road became a green tunnel to be driven very slow, one chuckhole at a time.

In the 1960s the loggers returned to cut the virgin forests on valley walls beyond reach of the old railroads. CCC Road was pretty much abandoned, replaced on the valley floor by a Middle Fork Road that, opened to the public, made CCC Road that much lonesomer. Then the log-export industry got in gear and the Second Wave clearcutters of the second-growth put it to work to assist in reskinning the moraines and cleaning up "long corners" of virgin forest. By the late 1980s the indus-

Pratt River Valley from CCC truck road

try had gone about as far as it could go. Again CCC Road fell silent.

Excellent! The hour has struck to advance the CCC crusade beyond the decadence of gasoline nightmares to transcendent consummation—a motorfree trail. It can be done. Indeed, the installation of a car-barring gate in the late 1980s already has done the deed on a temporary basis. Three steps must be taken by King County/DNR/U.S. Forest Service: (1) Determine the legal status of the road (if it crosses any private land, 60 years of unobstructed public use surely have given the public adverse possession); (2) decide which one or two or three governmental units should take responsibility; and (3) get on with formally establishing the route as a trail and firmly excluding motors.

The thought already exists in at least one governmental mind. Mt. Baker–Snoqualmie National Forest is drawing lines on the map. A trail is envisioned from Mt. Si Road, following CCC Road to where it starts the descent toward old Camp Brown, new construction to carry feet onward at the mid-elevation level to the Taylor River. Day-walks. Creekside picnic spots. Pretty little trail camps. Sidetrails from the valley bottom to the ridges. A whole new recreational world founded on labors of the New Deal CCC.

West Entry

*One way from the gate to Big Blowout Creek 5½ miles (from Brawling
    Creek, 2¼ miles)*
High point 1520 feet, elevation gain 220 feet, loss 240 feet
All year

Drive Mt. Si Road through post–tree-farming suburbia to the turnoff to Mount Teneriffe (described earlier in this chapter). At School Bus Turnaround is a sign, "Road Closed—Do Not Enter." This illegal "bluff" sign is not to be totally ignored. The way leaves pavement and steeply climbs 0.9 mile to the far frontier of exurbia at 1300 feet. Here the road splits in three. The left ascends to homes; the middle, the original CCC Road, dwindles to an impassable naught; the right, the replacement road, is gated. *Do not park here.* There's not enough room and the folks up the left fork have been rumored to do bad things to road-blocking cars. Backtrack down the hill to harmless (and safe) parking.

A note to planners of the CCC Trail-to-be: The gate is welcome but not at the 1994 site. The road ought to be opened 1 more mile to the leveling-out atop the moraines. Until the new trees leap up, the views will continue to be enormous over the Middle Fork valley, which served as trough for both the valley glacier that flowed from the Cascade

Crest and the ice sheet that invaded from Canada; to the North Bend Plain and Rattlesnake; over Grouse Ridge to the South Fork valley framed by Mailbox/Garcia and Washington; over the Middle Fork to clearcuts of Granite Creek, Teneriffe, Green, and scalped Bessemer; and to the rugged Russian Buttes and the Yosemite-like granite walls of Garfield. A worthy sidetrip, indeed, for family picnickers doing the Greenway.

As of 1994 the hiker must puzzle through a maze of logging roads old and new. Which was the original CCC Road? By pursuing the self-evidently correct direction (checking the map), an alert person can avoid superfluous mistakes. At 2.6 miles from the gate is the turnoff to Green Mountain; the gate might quite properly be here, or 0.5 mile farther, at Brawling Creek, 1520 feet, where a road-end picnic area and self-guiding nature trail would be great favorites.

Brawling Creek is first in a series of watercourses that regularly flush winter cloudbursts and spring snowmelt from logger-skinned slopes and rip out the road. Jeeper engineers used to do annual repairs for the exhilaration of proving the mastery of their wheels over Nature, but Nature has pretty well stifled their ya-hooing. Indeed, a few spots are tight squeaks for a hiker. Horses have given up entirely.

At ⅓ mile from Brawling Creek is a skinny ledge blasted across a wall of granite slabs polished smooth by the ice. Big views, never to be blocked by forest because the ledge is at the edge of empty air. Masses of logs avalanched from clearcuts can make progress over and under the jackstraw, along the brink, distinctly perilous. In ⅔ mile more, at a very unruly creek, slabs end at the gigantic logging show of the 1970s which has made the creek so unruly. In the next 1⅓ miles are broad views, more demented creeks, and finally Big Blowout Creek, 1280 feet. Destabilized by clearcutting near the summit of Bessemer, the stream flows sometimes in a canyon a dozen feet deep, sometimes through a tumble of boulders, and sometimes down the connector road toward the valley road.

Middle Entry

One way from Big Blowout Creek to Tall Moss Cliff 1⅓ miles
High point 1520 feet, elevation gain 300 feet, loss 170 feet
All year

Drive Middle Fork Road (see "Middle Fork Snoqualmie River to Snoqualmie Pass") 5 miles from Vallley (*sic*) Camp and turn left on the unsigned Bessemer road, which climbs the moraines 1.1 miles to intersect CCC Road at Big Blowout Creek. The connector road is sometimes blown out by Big Blowout and sometimes is submerged in slumps of glacier-lakebed clay. It ought to be gated at the valley road and closed to public wheels.

This middle entry is better-liked by hikers than the west. From Big Blowout to Brawling, the section of the western sector that has the most interest, the distance is 2¼ miles, 3 miles of clearcuts less than from the west-end gate. Additionally, ⅓ mile to the east the Bessemer sideroad (gated) is passed and thereafter CCC Road definitely and finally has been converted to CCC Trail by sloughing of the denuded valley wall. As late as the middle 1980s, the surveyor's VW beetle could slip through but a few more winters brought that to a halt.

The way east tunnels young conifer forest, emerges to alder, crosses a saddle in a spur ridge, rounds a rock corner, and at 1 mile from the Bessemer road comes to a tall moss cliff and, below it, a prom-

Mount Garfield rising above the confluence of Taylor River and Middle Fork Snoqualmie River, from Green Mountain

ontory, 1350 feet. The winter views through the alder screen are superb 500 vertical feet down to the river, out the valley to the lowlands, up the valley to Garfield's cliffs, and across to Mount Roosevelt and the Pratt River valley, guarded by the beetling crags of Russian Buttes.

East Entry

One way from Middle Fork Road to Tall Moss Cliff 2 miles
High point 1450 feet, elevation gain 400 feet
All year

Drive Middle Fork Road (see "Middle Fork Snoqualmie River to Snoqualmie Pass") 2.3 miles beyond the Bessemer connector and spot a growing-in sideroad uphill left. Until the mid-1980s it was signed "CCC Road 1"—odd, because this *is* CCC Road, elevation 960 feet.

The sign is gone. Four-wheelers drive ⅓ mile and turn off right on a gypo logging road. They could not proceed straight ahead if they tried because in a hundred feet is a magnificent giant wheelstopper. (The bright side of man's mauling the mountains on a geologic scale of violence is that geological violence by Nature must ensue for many centuries to restabilize mountainsides. Roads become trails.)

The road-that-was narrows to a delightful footpath-that-is through groves of alder and half-century-old second-growth, the forest floor a carpet of moss. In 1 mile begin wintertime views across the Middle Fork to the Pratt. In a scant 2 miles, the way passes Tall Moss Cliff to the 1450-foot saddle, ½ mile and many fine wheelstoppers from the Bessemer road.

Green Mountain
(Map—page 105)

Round trip 7 miles, allow 6 hours
High point 2900 feet, elevation gain 1700 feet
February–December

The next mountain east from Teneriffe is Green. The 4824-foot summit presently lacks a trail and thus is pretty much left alone. However, the road-trail to a promontory is the Middle Fork Snoqualmie's best mid-elevation broad-view walk.

Walk CCC Truck Road Trail (described earlier in this chapter) 2.6 miles from the gate at 1300 feet. At 1514 feet turn left on a sideroad that climbs 0.1 mile to a Y. Go right, over a creek, to another Y. Take the right fork.

At 1 mile from CCC Trail, 2300 feet, a big ravine opens a wide-angle view down to the U-shaped glacier trough of the Middle Fork, the rolling moraine ridges out in the trough, and buttresses of Russian Buttes. The creek sheets over granite slabs, suggesting foot-washing and other water sports.

In four more switchbacks, at 2 miles, 2900 feet, the road-trail nears the top of the old clearcut and commences contouring. Here, beside an esthetic granite outcrop, is Far Enough Promontory. Sit on a granite bench thoughtfully provided by Nature and gaze out the valley to Rattlesnake and Rainier, across to Mailbox/Garcia and Russian Buttes and the mind-boggling clearcuts in Granite Creek, and up the valley to the Pratt River and the granite walls of Garfield, where Yosemite-like rock-climbers would throng if they could get a California-like audience.

Perhaps continue the contour another ¼ mile to Absolute Last Promontory, 2800 feet, and a close look at close-shaved Bessemer. Perhaps puzzle out the linkage of logging roads and keep going to Bessemer and loop on back via CCC Trail.

South Bessemer Mountain
(Map—page 105)

Round trip from CCC Truck Road Trail 9½ miles, allow 8 hours
High point 5000 feet, elevation gain 3800 feet
April–October

Thanks to its eminence as the apex of the ridge that starts with Mount Si and continues through Teneriffe and Green, and thanks to savage logging, South Bessemer is the supreme grandstand of the Middle Fork. The devastation is hideous—the Forest Service cringes and reminds the visitor, "Don't blame us, blame the Northern Pacific Land Grant, blame private industry." At lower elevations the second-growth since 1950's clearcutting is doing well enough. On high the 1970's clearcutting is a catastrophe on the geologic scale. Trees 450 years old and only as big as lowland trees grow in 30 years were cut—and fewer than a third were hauled away, the rest left to rot. Streams destabilized by the logging have gone crazy, flushing the mountain's soil to the valley in blowout floods.

Drive Middle Fork Road (see "Middle Fork Snoqualmie River to Snoqualmie Pass") 5 miles from Vallley (*sic*) Camp and turn left on the unsigned, rude, and often undrivable connector road 1.1 miles to CCC Truck Road Trail. Turn right 0.3 mile to a Y at elevation 1280 feet. Park here if not earlier.

Ascend left on the (gated) Bessemer road. At 2500 feet, 2 miles from CCC Trail, the way abruptly emerges from 1950s second-growth into 1970s stumpland and the views become flabbergasting.

To summarize the views: Early on the feature is the broad trough of the Middle Fork and the intricate dissection of the bed of the Pleistocene lake dammed by the glacier from Canada. Next the broad

Middle Fork Snoqualmie River valley and mountains in Alpine Lakes Wilderness from Bessemer Mountain

trough of the Pratt River dominates, the catkin-brown (in spring) lines of alder in green second-growth forest plainly showing the logging-railroad grades of the 1920s and 1930s. Then the "Low Sierra" walls of Garfield capture the eye, and the row of icy peaks on the Cascade Crest from Daniel to Chimney Rock to Lemah, and smaller peaks of the Snoqualmie Pass area. Finally there is the around-the-compass panorama from the summit—Rainier and Baker, the Olympics and Puget Sound and towers of downtown Seattle, Cougar Mountain, and the Snoqualmie River valley. No trees get in eyes' way.

Though the network of logging roads on Bessemer looks formidably intricate from a distance, there's no confusion. Always choose the option that proceeds meaningfully upward and you can't miss. At about 2 miles from the 2500-foot level, the main road comes within a few feet of a 4000-foot saddle. Keep to the main road 1 final mile to the scalped, bulldozed-flat top of South Bessemer Mountain at 5000 feet. A stone's throw away is the 5028-foot tippy-top whose patch of scrawny trees presumably was left to seed the crop of the year 3000. North Bessemer, 5166 feet, is a rough mile away. No stroll, that. But check out the possible connections in the other direction, to Green.

Taylor River
(Map—page 105)

Round trip (with sidetrips) 8⅔ miles, allow 5 hours
High point 2000 feet, elevation gain 800 feet
March–November

A road-trail wide enough for side-by-side sociable sauntering, a forest partly half-century-old second-growth and partly centuries-old old-growth, and, best of all, a series of creeks brawling and splashing down granite slabs from pool to pool.

Drive Middle Fork Road (see "Middle Fork Snoqualmie River to Snoqualmie Pass") 9.7 miles from Vallley (*sic*) Camp to the Taylor River bridge. At the Y just beyond go left, straight ahead, 0.5 mile to a firmly gated recrossing of the Taylor, elevation 1200 feet.

Walk Taylor River Road-Trail ⅓ mile to a Y. The Quartz Creek road goes off left and steeply up, climbing to clearcuts at 4000 feet and above (with very pretty scenery and a well-worn trail to Lake Blethen). Take the right fork. The river tumbles along close below, accessible by short sidetrips. Peaks of Garfield soar sharply high. The varied thrush

Otter Falls

Canadian dogwood, or bunchberry

trills, the winter wren twitters. The forest floor is carpeted with deer fern, elkhorn moss, teaberry, and bunchberry. Massive granite blocks invite scrambling.

At 2½ miles is the first of the big creeks, Marten, the falls churning a pool of limeade. For the best experience—actually, the hike climax— find a mean little old trail 100 feet before the plank bridge and climb through ancient cedars, some more than 12 feet in diameter. Take careful sidetrips for close views of a whole series of superb cataracts and plunge basins and clouds of spray.

Return to the road-trail for another 1¼ miles to Otter Falls, then ½ mile more to the concrete bridge over Big Creek, 1700 feet, and more falls, snow water sheeting down smooth granite. This is a neat spot to eat lunch, visualizing otters sliding the slabs.

If more exercise is wanted, Snoqualmie Lake is a couple of long, steep miles away at 3147 feet in the Alpine Lakes Wilderness.

From the North Bend Plain to the Cascade Crest: The North Ridge

Green Trails maps: Bandera, Snoqualmie Pass

Two valleys, of two distinct and very different rivers, descend west to the North Bend Plain from the Cascade Crest. The largest and longest is the Middle Fork Snoqualmie, many square miles in size and except for the Alpine Lakes Wilderness headwaters almost entirely abandoned to the motor sports and gun sports that overpower and expel quieter recreations. Justice to folks who prefer the sound of water to that of exploding hydrocarbons and the aroma of flowers to the reek of exhaust fumes requires that the lower valley, where spring comes early and summer stays late, be provided aplenty of water-play areas and family picnic spots and self-guiding nature paths. The U.S. Forest Service seems to have taken due if belated notice and is thought to be drawing up long-range plans for non-violent recreation.

Justice to the longer-legged hiker is expected to be done by a trail from the North Bend Plain to the highlands. In 1993 Gateway Bridge was built over the Middle Fork near Taylor River. The trail will go upvalley to the Cascade Crest, downvalley to the Pratt River trail, a link to Snoqualmie Pass. Other Forest Service thinking envisions extending the trail to the North Bend Plain, utilizing CCC Truck Road Trail (see the preceding). Other thinking by independent pedestrians aims toward reopening abandoned trails, constructing new ones, providing non-conflicting bikeways on logging roads no longer needed for that purpose (no more trees), and bringing family-friendly law and order to the Wild West.

The South Fork Snoqualmie is the "Main Street of the Northwest," corridor of electricity, natural gas, electronic communications, and a googol of thunderwagons and assorted wheels, yet on any given day populated by perhaps more feet in motion for the pure fun of it than all the roller rinks in the Northwest; note the number of trailheads described in these pages.

Dividing the two valleys is the "North Ridge," which begins in a quick lift from the Canadian moraines to the portal peak of Mailbox/ Garcia and continues to Defiance, Bandera, Granite, and Snoqualmie

Freeway from Dirty Harry's Balcony

Pass. The Snoqualmie Pass peaks have been popular since The Mountaineers built their Snoqualmie Pass Lodge in 1914 and got up two lists, ten each, of Snoqualmie Lodge Pin Peaks. At least until the 1940s, earning the two "Snoqualmie pins" was a milepost on the journey to the "Six Majors Pin" and, after that, who could say? Everest was not climbed until 1953.

However, for every climber who stood atop a Snoqualmie Pass peak, perhaps a thousand male lads strangled on the smoke of wet wood at camps on the shores of the "Boy Scout Lakes" west of the pass. Eventually the bathing suit was added to mandatory trip gear, acknowledging that females had quit fainting and begun sweating and that the wilderness rain blesses all sexes indiscriminately.

It has been left to the present generation to understand the need for fuller recreational exploitation of the North Ridge. A North Ridge Trail. More access trails to it. More backcountry camps. The portion of the North Ridge in the Alpine Lakes Wilderness will have to be more and more carefully protected against the crush of too much love. But it would be bitter irony if the nation's glad acceptance of the wilderness vision caused a decrease in the availability of wilderness experience. The Wilderness wilderness must be forever wild; in the words of Thoreau, "in wildness is the preservation of the world." The portion of the North Ridge outside the Alpine Lakes Wilderness is wildland now and must so remain; though most of it might rate only 7 or so on a wilderness scale of 10, that is ample to give spiritual balm; more people seeking such balm can be served by more low-impact (low-speed, low-decibel) trails and "hardened" backcountry camps (architect-plotted tent sites, privies, perhaps even wells operated by manual pump).

The noise of motors and the speed of machines will continue undiminished on Main Street; traffic on the alley trails should be slow enough for the hiker's eye to admire each flower and never louder than the shriek of a little child meeting a garter snake.

Middle Fork Snoqualmie River to Snoqualmie Pass
(Map—page 128)

One way from Middle Fork Road to Snoqualmie Pass about 22 miles, allow 3 days (Stan did it in 1½ days)
High point 5280 feet, elevation gain about 7500 feet
July–October

To know the "greater ecosystem" of a mountain range, walk (don't run, don't wheel) from the front to the middle. A meadow of alpine flowers, a torrent roaring from a glacier, a rock spire poking the sky in the eye can be experienced in isolation by, for example, a half-hour tour in a helicopter taxi. (Pay your $100, take home a video show for folks in the neighborhood.) However, a *respectful* approach is required to know these not as pretty little bits but parts of the whole.

Several routes are described in these pages for potential trails from the North Bend Plain to the Cascade Crest and all will be built, someday. But one has been an on-the-ground reality for a century or so. In 1975, to publicize the campaign for a Sound to Mountains Trail,

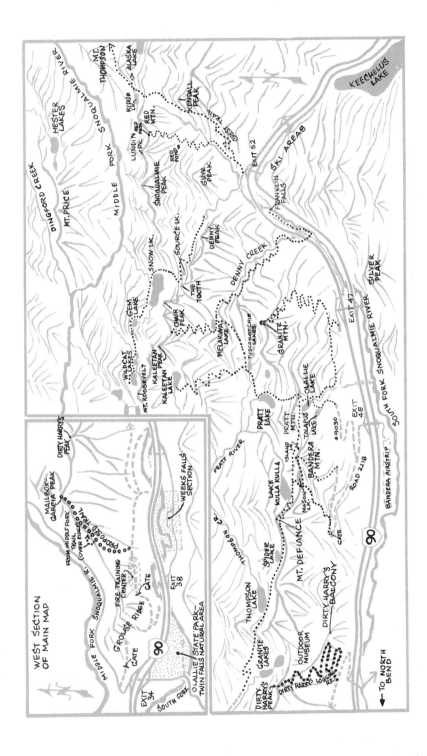

Stan Unger walked this venerable route as the conclusion of his foot journey that began at West Point in Seattle's Discovery Park. In 1981 it was walked in the opposite direction by the Mountains to Sound March organized by The Mountaineers and led by Jim Whittaker to protest Secretary of the Interior Watt's announced intention to issue leases to generate geothermal power in the Alpine Lakes Wilderness; the climaxing rally at Seattle's Gasworks Park was the largest assemblage of environmentalists in the history of the Northwest.

Go off I-90 on Exit 34, signed "Edgewick Road," turn left under the freeway, pass Seattle East Auto Truck Plaza, and turn right on Middle Fork Road. The paved road splits in two pieces which rejoin at the far frontier of exurbia and the end of pavement at Vallley (*sic*—Lutheran Laymen's League) Camp, 2.1 miles from the turn onto Middle Fork Road. In 0.3 mile is a sprawl of roadside gravel, entry to three roads. Take the far left, paralleling Middle Fork Road without gaining elevation. In 0.3 mile is a Y, the left to a deadend. Take the right, uphill, a few yards to an ever-locked gate you failed to see from the Y. Back up to park at the Y, elevation 800 feet.

The road ascends mixed forest, views occasional to valley and moraine, Rattlesnake to Si to Bessemer. A nice short walk in early spring when the heights are dreary white. At 1700 feet, 2½ miles from the gate, the way turns sharp right into Granite Creek valley, crosses the creek, and ascends 1½ miles to a Y at 2800 feet. Take the left a scant ½ mile to a second Y, 3100 feet. The right fork contours to Granite Lakes, both logged to the shores in the 1970s, when this sort of savagery was legal and usual; take the left and shortly switchback left. In a bit is a junction where the bigger road proceeds straight ahead out onto the ridge whose nakedness is an interstate embarrassment; take the right, a rude and ruined track. No sign. In about ½ mile is a Y; take the right, possibly signed "Mt. Defiance Trail." In a long zigzagging ⅓ mile the road switchbacks left to a berm blockade. Off the spur to the right, perhaps marked by fragments of an old sign, "Mt. Defiance," true trail begins. Navigation now becomes possible for travelers of less than supernatural skill.

The trail leaves clearcut and climbs to a forested 4300-foot saddle 5½ miles from the gate. A descent to Thompson Lake, 3680 feet, and an ascent to Defiance Ridge, 4800 feet, lead in some 3 miles from the last of the Granite Creek road to a sidehill of Mount Defiance at 5280 feet, close below the 5584-foot summit.

Other trips in these pages describe the drop of the trail to Mason Lake, 4300 feet, and the alternative continuations this way and that. The classic line of the Sound to Mountains Trail tours the Boy Scout

Lakes (to repeat for emphasis, the surveyor himself being a radical feminist who wants women to be allowed in military combat but not men, they are called that because of a past era when Girl Scouts were not permitted in wildlands unless accompanied by parents or certified chaperones). Rainbow, Pratt, and Lower Tuscohatchie. Sidetrails to Kulla Kulla, Mason, Island, Olallie, Talapus, Windy, and Kaleetan. At some 7 miles from Defiance is Melakwa Lake, 4550 feet. The trail crosses Hemlock Pass, 4600 feet, and follows Denny Creek down to Denny Creek Campground, 2300 feet, 4½ miles from the Melakwa outlet.

Denny Creek Road (old Snoqualmie Pass Wagon Road-Highway) ascends in some 1½ miles to Snoqualmie Pass, 3004 feet, 93 miles from West Point as measured by Stan's hot feet.

Mailbox/Garcia Peak
(Map—page 131)

Round trip 12 miles, allow 10 hours
High point 4841 feet, elevation gain 4000 feet
March–November

On either side of the gateway from the North Bend Plain to the upper South Fork Snoqualmie stand portal peaks. On the south is Washington, the name old and established. Its companion on the north had no name this surveyor could discover when he commenced *Footsore* explorations in 1976; he referred to it provisionally as "West Defiance." By whatever name, or none, it cried out for boots. The summit views obviously were the equal of Si's. The upper slopes could be seen from the valley to be snowfree in April or even March, while trails farther east were plugged up until June. Thanks to nineteenth century fires that destroyed the forest, and rock outcrops that won't let seedlings root, and the hot sun of a southwest exposure that shrivels the shrubs, the hiking season is very long for a peak so high. Additionally, the subalpine meadows probably are Seattle's closest. Having other infidels to attend to himself, the surveyor preached up a crusade for "a group of doughty volunteers" to whack out a trail from Grouse Ridge. (More of this later.)

Imagine this surveyor's amazement in 1991 to read *Signpost Magazine* letters by Sally Pfeiffer describing a trail to the summit, for which she coined the name "Mailbox" because the register book was inside a very old, heavy, green mailbox. Who carried it up there?

When? Notes in the box dated to the 1950s; Sally estimates the trail was built no later than 1940.

Ignorant of this, the surveyor meanwhile had decided the peak had to have a better name than "West Defiance" and nominated "Dirty Harry's Peak." He quickly deferred to Sally's suggestion that this name belonged to the peak Harry Ault had scalped. The question remains, does "Mailbox" hold the historical high ground? Most likely, though there seems to have been some use, somewhere, of "Garcia," after a settlement below Dirty Harry's Balcony, which was wiped out by I-90. Who was "Garcia"? The Cuban whose "Message To" was the subject of an inspirational essay-oration from the Spanish-American War? A brand of cigars favored by an encampment of railroad workers? The final decision may have to be left to a higher court.

Drive to Vallley (*sic*) Camp (see "Middle Fork Snoqualmie River to Snoqualmie Pass") and 0.3 mile beyond to the wide gravel entry to three roads on the right. Take the middle road, its yellow gate always locked except when logs are being hauled, so don't drive it. Park below the gate, elevation 800 feet.

Note: This trail is not for everyone: It is rough and varies from steep to very steep to awful steep, and a 4000-foot elevation gain is horrendous for 1 day. But the view is wide and grand from Russian Butte to Glacier Peak.

The day of the trailhead survey, the gate happened to be open, and for the sake of precise mileage the road was driven. In 0.2 mile a road

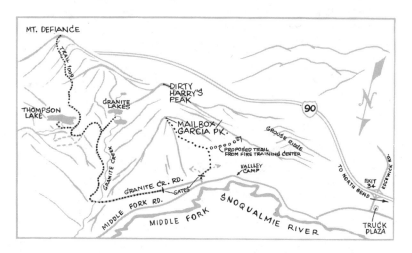

climbs left; keep straight ahead. At 0.3 mile from Middle Fork Road pass the trailhead. (If a small stream is passed, go back 75 feet.)

"Pass" is the word. Don't expect to see a boulevard. Or anything except maybe a blue or pink ribbon or two. Step off the edge of the road and find tread with your feet. When you spot a wood sign hidden behind a tree to the right, "4841," you know you've got it—by George you've got it. (Clearcut signs indicate the beginning of the trail may be logged in the near future.)

The trail weaves through forest where Grouse Ridge merges into Mailbox Peak. The trail crosses several streams and, before the hillside steepens, crosses to the left side of the valley and turns abruptly upward. (Watch carefully for the true trail because game trails and surveyor's ribbons also go up Grouse Ridge.) The trail climbs steeply to the end of decent tread where the forest also ends. Exiting to the right onto semi-naked slopes of the ancient burn, the way is marked by rib-

Mailbox Peak; the flag was up, but the postman hadn't picked up the mail all winter

bons through shrub-trees, beargrass, and huckleberries to the ridge crest. A small felsenmeer-rockslide and a field of heather lead to the mailbox, 4841 feet.

Warren Jones, longtime prominent member of the North Bend–area trail intelligentsia, informs us the trail originally started at Vallley (*sic*) Camp, implying the Lutherans probably were the builders. Clearcuts have obliterated this beginning stretch. The first mile of surviving trail may not survive the clearcuts now filling ships bound for Asia. We trust the volunteers will keep an eye on the chainsaws and when needed come with brushcutting tools and rolls of ribbon. Activists of the Middle Fork want to see this trailhead perpetuated and are trying to figure out which, if any, governmental agency can be awakened.

However, the surveyor's old suggestion for a trail from the top of Grouse Ridge still is valid. A peak this good easily can stand two starting points. From a trailhead at 1600 feet, by the State Fire Training Center, some ½ mile of new construction would intersect the summit trail (see "Grouse Ridge").

Grouse Ridge
(Map—page 128)

Round trip 4 miles, allow 3 hours
High point 1500 feet, elevation gain 1000 feet
All year

A highway traveler more than normally observant may wonder why a ridge crosses the South Fork Snoqualmie valley at right angles. Aren't ridges supposed to parallel valleys? Ah, says the geomorphologist, you reckon without the glaciers. This is a moraine marking a long-stable terminus of the ice, a dumping ground. Here, said early geologists, was the end of a glacier descending the South Fork Snoqualmie. However, a professor at the University of Washington, Dr. J. Hoover Mackin, was bothered by fractious evidence. To make a long scientific detective story short, he proposed the preposterous notion the glacier hadn't come down the valley but up. And he proved it. The moraine was none other than that of the ice sheet invading from Canada and pushing deep into the Cascades.

That's one fascinating thing about Grouse Ridge, as the moraine is called in this segment. The other is that it was on the route of the first road from the lowlands over Snoqualmie Pass. A construction start by Seattle pioneers in 1859 was aborted by the Civil War. In 1865 some $2500 was subscribed by boosters and a Snoqualmie Pass Trail or Wagon Road cleared nearly to the pass—though as late as 1872 an actual crossing by a wagon rated a newspaper item. Such Seattle entrepreneurs as A. A. Denny and H. L. Yesler realized the government wasn't going to help; in 1883 was organized the Seattle and Walla Walla Train and Wagon Road Company, which for a decade operated the Seattle–Walla Walla Toll Road, the first cross-Cascades road link between Seattle and Eastern Washington. But there wasn't much call for it when built, and even less after completion of the cross-mountain line of the Northern Pacific Railroad. In 1892 the 14-foot right-of-way was signed over to King County in a quit-claim deed. The county promptly commenced a long neglect, letting logs fall and creeks gully and weeds grow. But time was marching on, or wheeling on, and the nation was falling helplessly in love with new-fangled machines and in 1905 the first cars crossed Snoqualmie Pass. As a promotion event for the Alaska-Yukon-Pacific Exposition of 1909, an automobile race was held from New York to Seattle, requiring the over-mountains road to be made at least temporarily passable. Soon everybody was getting wheels, and in 1913 a primary highway, part of the transcontinental system, was designated over Snoqualmie Pass. However, Sunset Highway, formally opened in 1915, followed a new line east from North Bend, the line that remained in use until the coming in the 1970s of I-90. From 1931 it was kept open in winter and in 1934 it was paved, partly from the output of a concrete mixer into which this surveyor's father shoveled sand, gravel, and cement.

As traffic grew on what in the 1920s was called Yellowstone Trail or Highway (a reflection of the popularity of the national park as a goal for the new American sport of auto-touring), a 6.2-mile stretch of the pioneer route was forgotten. Loggers eventually reopened the road to haul logs and freeway-builders to haul gravel. Later, firemen moved in to take training. Resemblance to a wagon road is now slight but the view is basically what the pioneers saw, leaving aside the absence of forests and the presence of cities.

Go off I-90 on Exit 34, signed "Edgewick Road," turn left to pass under the freeway, and opposite the Seattle East Truck Plaza turn right on paved (sidewalks, even; somebody's got plans) 146th to a gate, elevation 650 feet.

The gate is never open to public wheels and a sign warns "Private Property." Yes, the land is private and no doubt fated for a New City but the road is public, freely open to feet.

The first scant 1 mile is virtually flat and totally clearcut and not replanted as a farm would be. Views are of Teneriffe, Si, Rattlesnake, Washington, and Mailbox/Garcia. Arriving at the moraine, the way turns up, switchbacking, narrowing. Dodge sideroads left and keep heading for the powerline. The main road goes under the powerline at 1350 feet, through up-leaping firs of a plantation to a clearcut of the early 1980s, and at 1500 feet, a scant 2 miles from the gate, comes to a promontory landing and the climax views. See the South Fork Snoqualmie below, in Twin Falls Natural Area, and look out to where the river plunges via Snoqualmie Falls from the old lakebed of the upper valley. See lanes of I-90, tree-mining clearcuts high on valley walls, smog of Puget Sound City. See Rattlesnake, Si, and Teneriffe. It's enough. Bring out the pickles and grapes and granola cookies and root beer. Listen for wagon wheels of immigrants. The moo-ing and baa-ing of beef and mutton walking from the Kittitas and Methow Valleys to

Freeway and Mount Si from Grouse Ridge

Seattle butchers. The putt-putt-bang of AYP road-racers. The Origi-nals on the way to attack the Newcomers on Puget Sound. The glacier dropping boulders.

The road tops out at 1600 feet in temporary forests on the flat pla-teau of Grouse Ridge. Sort through the confusion of roads by aiming for Mailbox/Garcia. Some 3½ miles from the lower gate, the walker bumps against a fence at the edge of a gravel pit which was a major source of raw material for I-90 and was visible to astronauts on the Moon. The fence is purely to stop playwheels and is readily walked around.

The view! The North Ridge from Mailbox/Garcia to Bandera, the South Ridge from Washington to McClellan Butte. This segment of the 1865 wagon road definitely must lie on the proposed low-speed Sunday Drive for family picnickers.

Beyond the fence (and its ever-locked gate), good gravel road skirts the awesome gravel pit, now occupied by the State Fire Training Cen-ter. In 0.2 mile from the fence, the road cuts the base of Mailbox/Garcia Peak at an elevation of 1600 feet. Here is where the volunteers should start a new ½-mile path to intersect the summit trail.

In 0.4 mile, having passed vistas of scurrying firemen and the fire-proof building to which they regularly set fire, the gravel road joins a paved road at the entry gate to the training center. The gate is not signed to exclude the public; even when closed, as presumably it some-times is, it can be walked around. In 1.8 miles more the entry road, paved but single-lane with turnouts, ideal for Sunday Driving, passes an obscure sideroad right, to the river, the conclusion of the 6.2 miles. Upvalley from here the old road has been obliterated by several eras of newer engineering. Yet the Sunday Drive can continue on the other side of the freeway on the log-haul road east and a connection to Denny Creek Road to Snoqualmie Pass.

Dirty Harry's Balcony
(Map—page 128)

Round trip 5 miles, allow 4 hours
High point 2550 feet, elevation gain 1300 feet
February–December

Driving I-90 along the South Fork Snoqualmie above the moraine, a person paying attention to more than concrete and machines notes that at a certain point the valley, quite wide upstream and down-

McClellan Butte from Dirty Harry's Balcony; lines of vegetation are alder and willow growing on abandoned logging roads

stream, is constricted by a ridge thrusting from the side of Defiance Ridge. A person with an eye for rock may look up and judge this a most impressive collection indeed of precipices and chimneys. If that person has a taste for pedestrian exercise, he/she may wonder what it's like to be up there on the top. Well, he/she ought to go find out. Ought to look down from bald buttresses, down and down more than 1000 exceedingly vertical feet, to a most impressive collection of concrete ribbons and busy machines. But the view down is only a fraction of the vista from "Dirty Harry's Balcony." Furthermore, in season the rock garden is a brilliance of blossoming herbs and shrubs.

Go off I-90 on the west entry to Exit 38 and follow signs, "State Fire Training Center," along old U.S. 10, now a rest-and-recreation boulevard that ends at a freeway underpass, the east entry to Exit 38. At 0.2 mile from the underpass is a gate, signed "Locked after 4 P.M.

Road ends 2.5 miles ahead. There is no other road out of the area" (little white lies; see "Grouse Ridge"). At 0.2 mile from the gate is a bridge over the South Fork Snoqualmie; this and several other water-play and picnic spots require the road to be made a Sunday Drive from North Bend direct, not via freeway. At 0.3 mile from the bridge is the gravel lane left to the river; more water-play, more history. In 0.1 mile more, on a curve and easy to miss, Dirty Harry's Logging Road, un-signed, climbs to the right. Just a trail now. And creekbed. Elevation, 1350 feet.

In 1½ miles, at 2500 feet, Dirty Harry's Logging Road switchbacks west. Go off right on a path to a saddle and campsite between Defiance Ridge slopes and Balcony Ridge. Just past the camp turn right and fol-low the path through snags of a silver forest, shrubs, and salal onto the mossy, craggy bald top of Dirty Harry's Balcony, 2550 feet.

Zounds! Look east to Bandera, south to McClellan Butte, west to Washington, and—from other viewpoints nearby—farther west to Rattlesnake, lower Snoqualmie Valley and the Olympics. But espe-cially look down the giddy crags to the concrete swath of I-90, where bugs chase each other's tails east and west, and to the gravel channels of the river, and to the abandoned railroad and the gashes of tree-mining roads that climb so high, almost touch the sky—and would be hauling logs from there, too, if Nature could grow trees on clouds and if there had been a Northern Pacific Cloud Grant to augment the domin-ions of free enterprise.

From the first bald top explore others, stepping very gingerly along the brink, admiring airy pillars and deep-incised chimneys and scary cliffs. In spring the knobs and pillars and chimneys and cliffs are a glowing garden of penstemon and paintbrush and beargrass and much more.

Dirty Harry's Peak
(Map—page 128)

Round trip 11 miles, allow 9 hours
High point 4650 feet, elevation gain 3400 feet
May–November (to lower points, March)

Among the surveyor's happiest accomplishments in *Footsore* ex-plorations was "discovering" Dirty Harry. Among the surveyor's great regrets is missing out on meeting (several times by mere minutes) the

McClellan Butte from Dirty Harry's Balcony

Quintessential Gypo, a Vanishing American. Who necessarily *must* vanish, but still....

The name he liked to be called by North Bend friends was "Dirty Harry." For many years his business and pleasure was purchasing the timber on private land and chainsawing scraggly, next-to-worthless forests to desolation, practicing logging methods subsequently outlawed, thanks in no small part to the horrors he committed in full view of the millions of travelers on the Main Street of the Northwest. He was the despair of the Forest Service and Weyerhaeuser, who bore the brunt of the anguished accusations by a citizenry ignorant of who had done the foul deed. He pushed his cats to the very summit of the 4650-foot peak of Defiance Ridge, which we have named for him.

From the switchback at 2500 feet on Dirty Harry's Logging Road, continue west 1¾ miles to a promontory at 2800 feet, far enough for an early-spring snowline-probing grip. Since Harry went away the alders have grown up thick as the hairs on a dog's back; the view through windows is across the valley to McClellan Butte, down to I-90 and river, east to Snoqualmie Pass peaks, and out the portals of the Cascade front to the lowlands.

A bit farther, at 3000 feet, the road crosses a tumbling creek, site of Dirty Harry's Museum, trucks and machines scavenged from junkyards and kicked and cussed up here for a final rusting place. Cat tracks climb into the creek valley and go off this way and that. Stick with the main track, plainly identified by the beating of many boots that know where they're going. At about 4000 feet the alder thins out and views grow opener and wider. At about 1½ miles from Museum Creek, the road tops out on the summit.

Count rings in the stumps of trees that had grown to little more than a foot in diameter. The counting is difficult, the rings are so close, and most of the trees were rotten at the core; Harry hauled only one in five to the mill, left the rest. One wonders where he found a mill that would even bother with mountain hemlock. One also wonders why he didn't bulldoze the heather and the beargrass.

Turn to the views. West beyond the final two peaks of Defiance Ridge (Peak 4926 and 4841-foot Mailbox/Garcia) are North Bend, Rattlesnake, Issaquah Alps, smog-dimmed towers of Seattle, the smoke pall of invisible Tacoma, Green Mountain (the one just west of Bremerton), and the Olympics. South, beyond Washington, is Rainier. North is Baker. Easterly are Kaleetan, Chair, Chimney, and that other volcano, Glacier Peak. Beyond the Middle Fork are the boggling clearcuts on Bessemer. Straight down the cliffs (watch your step) are the clearcut shores of Granite Lakes.

Mason Lake and Mount Defiance
(Maps—pages 128 and 131)

Round trip to Mason Lake 5 miles, allow 6 hours
High point 4300 feet, elevation gain 2200 feet
June–November
Round trip to Mount Defiance 10 miles, allow 10 hours
High point 5584 feet, elevation gain 3500 feet
July–October

Mason Lake is the quickest mountain lake from Seattle, and the trail looks so short on the map the novice hiker supposes it's easy. But the "trail" is the masterpiece of a Phantom Builder who embodied in his work just about every possible blunder in route and construction.

The Forest Service wishes it could learn the identity of the Phantom, not to press charges but to explain why his Good Deed is Bad. On a summer day this benefactor's chamber of horrors is a parade of day-hikers and dogs, young marrieds toting babes, and beginners fresh from the Co-op and laboring under loads of 1001 Essentials. But if Mason Lake is a C-minus (generous), Mount Defiance is an A-plus. Enormous views. Mountain meadows, very nearly the closest to Seattle.

Lake Kulla Kulla from Mount Defiance trail

Go off I-90 on Exit 45, cross under the freeway, and drive straight ahead on road No. 9030. At a split in 1 mile, go straight ahead on road No. 9031, signed "Mason Lake Way." At 3.8 miles from the freeway is a blockade. Park here, elevation 2100 feet.

Ascend the abandoned road a scant 1 mile to the torrent of Mason Creek. A bit beyond is the trail, which politely switchbacks until it has inveigled victims into the trap and then commences systematic torture. The creek, of course, is a symphony. The ancient forest is a joy forever. However, these are adequate compensation only when a person is not in motion. At about 1¼ miles the Phantom came to a boulder field where construction of a trail would demand more high explosive than was dropped on Dresden. Go slow. Be cautious. The big blocks are tricky, slippery when wet, and some teeter. Cairns and flags mark the best way and also the worst. Who can you trust? Not the Phantom. When the Forest Service gets funds, it will install a rational trail and warn against this one by placing a skeleton at the trailhead. It is hoped the Phantom will volunteer for this final Good Deed.

A conclusion of easy and pleasant forest leads into the basin and the shore of Mason Lake, 4300 feet, 2½ miles. If camps are crowded, try Little Mason Lake, off on a swampy sidetrail. Within a mile are four other lakes.

The peak calls. The trail climbs 200 feet in ½ mile to a junction on the ridge between Mason Lake and Lake Kulla Kulla. Ascend the ridge trail west on south slopes of Defiance. At 5200 feet, about 2 miles from the junction, a meadow is a glory of blossoms in early summer. A steep scramble up the west edge culminates in the summit, 5580 feet.

Gaze. Over the Middle Fork Snoqualmie to Baker and Glacier. Over the South Fork to Rainier and Adams and, on a smogfree day, what's left of Mount St. Helens. Five volcanoes, that's a lot.

Bandera Mountain
(Map—page 128)

Round trip 7 miles, allow 6 hours
High point 5240 feet, elevation gain 2800 feet
May–October

The easiest summit panoramas of the upper Greenway are from Bandera. Out the valley to Puget Sound and the Emerald City, into the Alpine Lakes Wilderness, up and down the length of the Cascades.

Mount Rainier from Bandera Mountain

Snow melts early on the southwesterly exposure, permitting bare-ground ascents while nearby peaks are still a white void. No patriarch trees shade delicate seedlings from the hostile sun. The summer of 1958 a fire started by loggers flued to timberline, which already was at low elevation because the upper slopes had been burned in the past century by Nature, as is Her right and obligation.

Drive road No. 9031 (see "Mason Lake and Mount Defiance") to the barricade, elevation 2100 feet.

Walk the abandoned road, passing the Mason Lake trail, 1½ miles to the end at a creek, the last chance to load canteens. (The stars at night are big and bright, the lights of Puget Sound City are a nova in the west, and headlights on I-90 are a tempting subject for a long-exposure photograph as a river of electricity.)

The surveyor takes personal pride in Bandera. He was on his way home from a missionary trip to Utah the day the firestorm blew up; an easterly wind carried smoke over Seattle, so darkening what had been a blue-sky, sun-bright morning that city folks supposed it was on-shore flow, rain soon to follow. Several years later he set out to explore over-looked hiking opportunities along the Greenway-to-be. His acquain-tance with Washington and Mailbox/Garcia began, sort of, as noted elsewhere in these pages. After many frustrations he found his way to the road-end at the creek. Accompanied by his 5-year-old Buddy Pal and the sheep dog with the piebald eyes, Natasha, he scrambled up slopes near the creek to the margin of the 1958 burn and clambered over dozens of charcoaled logs. (Said sad but wise Buddy Pal, "Daddy, you don't get no place 'sploring.") Only on the descent did he find the path whacked out along the edge of the burn by the Smokey Bears.

From the last black log, the way continued upward in beargrass and silver snags of the nineteenth century blazes. (After some 150 years there is not so much as the start of a new forest, vivid illustration of the scientific fact that logging at this elevation is not "tree-farming" but "timber-mining.") Mountain-wise Buddy Pal looked to a lichen-gray granite talus and confidently announced, "Marmots live there." Surveyor said, "Well, maybe conies." Conies did indeed squeak. But a marmot whistled too. Score one for the kid.

Crossing a small granite talus, the surveyor was astounded to find an isolated stretch of built trail. Who built it? When? Why? Where did it come from? Where did it go?

The surveyor wrote up the hike for *102 Hikes in the Alpine Lakes,* as the guidebook was called in that edition. Returning several years later, the scramble route pioneered by Buddy Pal, Natasha, and Daddy looked almost like a real trail. These 30 years later it is more so. The Forest Service blames the Phantom. But this path is no horror. Easy enough for a 5-year-old kid and a sheep dog with piebald eyes.

The ridge is attained at around 4700 feet, immediately above Ma-son Lake. (In the opinion of the surveyor, this over-the-mountain route is kinder and gentler than Mason Creek Way.) Views from the ridge are nearly as broad as those from the summit and the route this far often melts clean in early May.

Climb east on the crest through subalpine trees and scramble granite blocks up a ridge step to the first summit, 5050 feet, and down-and-up to the highest summit, 5240 feet. Look down to lakes in forest bowls, out north to Glacier Peak and Baker, northeasterly to Snoqualmie peaks, down south to the freeway and beyond to Rainier, and west past the portals of Washington and Mailbox/Garcia to Puget Sound. Civilization is near but so is wilderness.

Talapus and Olallie Lakes
(Map—page 128)

Round trip to Olallie Lake 4 miles, allow 3 hours
High point 3780 feet, elevation gain 1220 feet
June–October

A well-groomed forest trail, perfect for first-time backpackers and families with young hikers, leads to two popular lakes with excellent camps and gives access to many more, the area crisscrossed by trails providing infinite opportunity for exploration. Due to the proximity to Puget Sound City, weekenders should arrive early to secure a desirable camp—a weekly average of 425 hikers visit here throughout June, July, and August, mostly on weekends.

Talapus Lake

Go off I-90 on Exit 45, cross under the freeway, and continue straight ahead west 1 mile on road No. 9030 to a split. Go right, uphill, still on road No. 9030, for 2.4 miles to the end at Talapus Lake trail No. 1039, elevation 2560 feet.

The trail begins on an overgrown logging road through an old clearcut, enters forest shade, and in several gentle switchbacks and a long sidehill swing reaches a marshy area just below Talapus Lake. Paths here branch in several directions. The muddy track that stays on the north side of the lake's outlet stream leads to several secluded camps on the west shore. The driest and best maintained is the main trail, which crosses the outlet on a bridge and at 1¼ miles comes to Talapus Lake, 3200 feet. Forest camps virtually ring the lake.

The way continues, ascending over a rib ½ mile to meet the sidetrail down from the Pratt Lake trail; turn left ¼ mile to Olallie Lake, 3780 feet, completely wooded, the camps numerous.

To proceed, ascend either by the sidetrail or directly from the far end of Olallie Lake to the Pratt Lake trail. Meadows and views start immediately.

Pratt Lake
(Map—page 128)

Round trip to saddle 11½ miles, allow 8 hours
High point 4100 feet, elevation gain 2300 feet in, 700 feet out
July–October

Miles of deep forest and a lovely lake amid subalpine trees. A network of trails leads to other lakes and to meadow ridges and high views. From a basecamp hikers and fishermen can spend days exploring.

Go off I-90 on Exit 47, cross over the freeway, and turn west 0.2 mile to the trailhead parking area, elevation 1800 feet.

The first steep mile gains 800 feet in cool forest to a junction with the Granite Mountain trail; just beyond is a nice creek. Turn left and sidehill upward on a gentler grade in young forest, through patches of twinflower, Canadian dogwood, salal, and bracken, by many nurse logs, to Lookout Point, 3 miles, 3400 feet, a much-used camp.

At 3¾ miles is a short sidepath down to Talapus and Olallie Lakes. The main trail rounds the Olallie basin in open subalpine forest to a 4100-foot saddle, 4 miles, a logical turnaround point for day-hikers. Lots of huckleberries here in season, plus a view south to Mount

Pratt Lake trail

Rainier, and a junction with the Mount Defiance trail. The Pratt Lake trail switchbacks down a steep hillside of much mud, some of it covered with puncheon, flattens out and contours above the lake, then drops to the outlet, 5¾ miles, 3400 feet. The lake is so heavily used the Forest Service requests campers to stay elsewhere.

Now, for explorations. In a scant ½ mile from Pratt Lake is Upper Tuscohatchie Lake, 3400 feet, and a choice of three directions for wandering: A fishermen's path beats brush 1½ miles to Tuscohatchie Lake, 4023 feet. From the outlet of Upper Tuscohatchie, a trail ascends gently, then steeply, 3 miles, in trees with glimpses outward of alpine scenery, to 4500-foot Melakwa Lake. Also from the outlet of Upper Tuscohatchie, a less-used trail climbs northward to 4800 feet and drops past little Windy Lake to Kaleetan Lake, 3900 feet, 3½ miles. The way is entirely in forest with only occasional views over the Pratt River valley, but the lonesome lake has a splendid backdrop in the cliffs of Kaleetan Peak.

From the Olallie–Pratt saddle (see "Talapus and Olallie Lakes"), the Mount Defiance trail ascends westward through beargrass and heather and huckleberry meadows (fine views 1100 feet down to Lake Talapus) on the side of Pratt Mountain, whose 5099-foot summit is an easy scramble via huge boulder fields on the southwest side, passes Rainbow Lake (Island Lake lies ½ mile away on a sidepath and actually is a more rewarding objective than Pratt Lake), comes near Mason Lake, traverses high above Lake Kulla Kulla, and climbs past flower gardens almost to the summit of 5584-foot Defiance, about 3 miles.

Granite Mountain
(Map—page 128)

Round trip 8 miles, allow 8 hours
High point 5629 feet, elevation gain 3800 feet
July–October

The most popular summit trail in the Snoqualmie region, for good reason. Though the ascent is long and in midsummer can be blistering hot, the upper slopes are a delight of granite and flowers, and the panorama includes Mount Rainier south, Mount Baker and Glacier Peak north, Chimney Rock and Mount Stuart east, and googols of other peaks, valleys, and lakes.

This lovely mountain is a killer. In spring its sunny southwest shoulder melts free of snow very early, seeming to provide bare-trail access to the heights. But the trail doesn't stay on the shoulder; it crosses a gully where snow lingers late and where climax avalanches thunder nearly to the edge of the freeway, sometimes carrying the bodies of hikers who should have chosen Bandera instead.

Go off I-90 on Exit 47, cross over the freeway, and turn west 0.5 mile to the trailhead parking lot, elevation 1800 feet.

The first steep mile on the Pratt Lake trail gains 800 feet in cool forest to the Granite Mountain junction and a creek for resting. This may be the last water.

Go right from the 2600-foot junction, traversing in trees ½ mile, then heading straight up and up in countless short switchbacks on an open south slope where fires and avalanches have inhibited the growth of forest. (On sunny days start early to beat the heat.)

Granite Mountain Lookout and Mount Rainier

At 4000 feet the trail abruptly gentles and swings east across the avalanche gully—an area of potentially extreme danger perhaps through June. Hikers seeking the summit before July should be very wary of crossing this gully; better to be content with the already very nice views to the south over Snoqualmie Valley to Rainier.

Beyond the gully the trail sidehills through rock gardens, passing a waterfall (early summer only) from snows above, and then switchbacks steeply to grass and flowers, reaching the summit ridge at 5200 feet. In early summer the route beyond here may be too snowy for some tastes; if so, wander easterly on the crest for splendid views over the Snoqualmie Pass peaks, down to alpine lakes, and through the pass to Lake Keechelus.

The trail ascends westward in meadows, above cozy cirque-scoop benches, and switchbacks to the fire lookout, 5629 feet, 4 miles.

Denny Creek and Melakwa Lake
(Map—page 128)

Round trip to Melakwa outlet 9 miles, allow 6 hours
High point 4600 feet, elevation gain 2300 feet
Mid-July–October

The liveliest valley of the Snoqualmie Pass vicinity, a series of waterfalls fluming and splashing. Beyond is the most spectacular alpine scenery, snowfields and cliffs of Kaleetan, Chair, and Bryant Peaks rising above the little lake, one shore in forest, the other in rocks and flowers.

Go off I-90 on Exit 47 to Denny Creek Road, turn right, and continue 3 miles to Denny Creek Campground. Just past it turn left on a road over the river and follow it 0.2 mile, passing private homes, to the road-end parking area and trailhead, elevation 2300 feet.

The trail ascends moderately along Denny Creek in forest, passing under I-90, crossing the stream on a bridge at ½ mile and recrossing at 1 mile, 2800 feet, below water-smoothed slabs of a lovely cataract. The way leaves forest and strikes upward in avalanche greenery to Keekwulee Falls, 1½ miles.

The next ½ mile of tight switchbacks ascends around cliffs past Snowshoe Falls. By this time the majority of Sunday strollers have found precisely the perfect spot for a picnic.

The next comparably rich rewards are a good bit farther on. At 2 miles, 3500 feet, the path flattens out in the upper basin, shortly crosses the creek, goes from trees to brush to trees again, and switchbacks to wooded Hemlock Pass, 3½ miles, 4600 feet. From here the trail drops a bit in forest to the outlet of Melakwa Lake, 4½ miles, 4550 feet.

Enjoy views of talus, snowfields, and cliffs falling abruptly from

Denny Creek

the 6200-foot summits of Kaleetan and Chair. The basin is so heavily pounded it's best not to camp in it at all even if permitted.

Franklin Falls
(Map—page 128)

Round trip 2, 1, or ½ miles, allow an hour to a day
High point 2600 feet, elevation gain none to hardly any
July–October

The most watery-exciting, history-fascinating, ancient-forested, family-style walk of the Greenway. Joan Burton, in *Best Hikes with Children in Western Washington and the Cascades*, says, "A paradise for kids! Standing beside the 70-foot falls on a warm day, they scream with joy at the cold spray in their face." But that's not the half of it. The Snoqualmie Pass Wagon Road described elsewhere in these pages (see "Grouse Ridge") lives on after a century and a third. We surveyors recall when this was our family route to the Mysterious East; little children who suppose I-90 was the Lord's project on the eighth day goggle at the rude track and openly think we're having them on, telling them it was possible to have an America with highways like this. There are grand old trees. Traces of prospect holes which were expected to disgorge riches to establish the Pittsburgh of the West. But there's more: cryptic numbers on survey stakes exhibit the survival of the American miner mentality. They are made by private enterprisers who seek to lay claim to the public waters. The proposed "Upper South Fork Snoqualmie Hydro Project" would shrivel Franklin Falls to a dribble, piping the river underground to a powerhouse below Denny Creek campground. Pipeline and power line would be added to the scenery. A section of corduroy road dating from the 1860s–1870s would be destroyed. Explain this to your kids, if you can.

Drive I-90 to Exit 47. Cross to the north side of the freeway and turn right on Denny Creek Road. At two miles, pass Denny Creek Campground, and a bit further the Snoqualmie Pass Wagon Road starts a 1-mile climb to Franklin Falls. The walk comes in three versions: short, shorter, and shortest. The 1-mile Franklin Falls Trail sets off from the other side of the road. Continue 0.4 mile up road No. 58 for the ½-mile route to the falls, 0.5 mile more for the ¼-mile trail.

Franklin Falls

Snow Lake
(Map—page 128)

Round trip to Snow Lake 7 miles, allow 6 hours
High point 4400 feet, elevation gain 1300 feet in, 400 feet out
July–October

Snow Lake is the largest alpine lake (more than a mile long) near Snoqualmie Pass. On one side cliffs rise steeply to Chair Peak and on the other forests fall steeply to the broad, deep gulf of the Middle Fork Snoqualmie River. The trail and lake are overwhelmingly popular—

Snow Lake

some 14,000 visitors a year, 500 and more on a fine summer Sunday. If it's the sound of silence you're seeking, be warned.

Go off I-90 on Exit 52 at Snoqualmie Pass and drive left 2 miles on the Alpental road through the ski area and subdivision to the parking lot and trailhead, elevation 3100 feet.

The trail climbs a bit in forest to intersect the one-time hiking route from the pass, obliterated by Alpental subdividers, and ascends gradually, sometimes in trees, sometimes on open slopes with looks over the 3800-foot droplet of Source Lake (the source of the South Fork Snoqualmie River) to Denny Mountain, now civilized, and to The Tooth and Chair Peak, still wild.

The way swings around the valley head and switchbacks a steep ½ mile in heather and flowers and parkland to the saddle, 3½ miles, 4400 feet, between Source Creek and Snow Lake. Not until here is the Alpine Lakes Wilderness entered. Day-hikers may well be content with the picnic spots in blossoms and blueberries and splendid views. The trail drops sharply ½ mile to meadow shores of Snow Lake, 4 miles, 4016 feet, and rounds the north side.

To provide the highest possible quality of experience without limiting the number of visitors, the Forest Service has devised a management plan for Snow Lake—a plan that informs hikers about "the Responsibility of Freedom." Within a "day-use area" along the shore first reached by trail, hikers are asked not to camp. In the adjoining "heavy-use area," camping should be at established sites only; no wood fires, carry a stove.

More lakes, more private, lie beyond. Walk the shore ½ mile to where the Rock Creek trail plummets to the Middle Fork and a bit more to the creek, the lake's outlet. Cross on a logjam. In 1 mile is Gem Lake, 4800 feet. The path rounds the east shore, climbs a 5000-foot pass, and drops 1000 feet to the two Wildcat Lakes.

Commonwealth Basin–Red Pass
(Map—page 128)

Round trip to pass 10 miles, allow 5 hours
High point 5400 feet, elevation gain 2700 feet in, 250 feet out
Mid-July–October

Hikers sorrowed by the half-century civilizing of Snoqualmie Pass tend not to go there anymore. Too much pain. However, diehard veter-

Picking blueberries at Red Pass; Mount Thompson in distance

ans of the war to save Commonwealth Basin from yo-yos and yodels suffer the anger for the sake of the triumph—peaceful subalpine forest, rippling creeks, an enclave of "olden days" ideal for a family picnic or experimental backpack.

Go off I-90 on Exit 52 at Snoqualmie Pass to the Alpental road and Pacific Crest Trail parking lot, elevation 3004 feet.

The ancient and honorable trail entered the basin in 1 mile, but on private land that ultimately was clearcut, causing the old path to erode so severely it was abandoned. The new way takes 2¾ miles and in the doing gains 700 feet, of which 250 are lost. Progress.

Follow the Pacific Crest Trail 2¾ miles, to where it dips near the basin floor before starting up Kendall Peak. A signed sidepath, trail No. 1033, drops to the old Commonwealth Basin trail. Go left or right for picnics—or for camps to try out brand-new gear or new kids.

The basin trail turns upstream 1 mile to the valley head and ascends the crest of an open-forested spur in many, many short switchbacks. The way flattens in the heather gardens and subalpine trees of a cirque at the foot of Red Mountain. A few steps away on a sidetrail is Red Pond, 4½ miles, 4900 feet. Eat lunch, tour the bouldery and flowery shores, listen for marmots whistling, walk to the edge of the cirque, and look over the valley and the rimming peaks and south to Mount Rainier. No camping; the scene is too fragile.

The trail swings up talus and rock buttresses almost but not quite to the ridge crest and sidehills west to Red Pass, 5 miles, 5400 feet, and views to the deep Middle Fork Snoqualmie valley, the sharp tower of Mount Thompson, the rugged Chimney Rock group, and far horizons.

This used to be the official Cascade Crest Trail and descended from the pass to the Middle Fork Snoqualmie River trail; a doughty soul might do it yet; proposals have been made that it be reopened for hikers only moderately doughty.

Kendall Katwalk
(Map—page 128)

Round trip to Katwalk 10½ miles, allow 7 hours
High point 5400 feet, elevation gain 2700 feet in, 300 feet out
Mid-July–mid-October

The bag of superlatives is quickly exhausted on this, one of the most spectacular parts of the Cascade section of the Pacific Crest Trail, and among the most accessible and popular.

Go off I-90 on Exit 52 at Snoqualmie Pass to the Alpental road and the Pacific Crest Trail parking lot, elevation 3004 feet.

The trail ascends forest 2 miles, loses 250 feet to negotiate a boulder field, and at 2¾ miles passes the connector to the Commonwealth Basin trail. Flattening briefly, the way switchbacks endlessly upward,

Kendall Katwalk

at 4300 feet crosses an all-summer creek that may be the last water until Ridge Lake, and at 4700 feet attains the wooded crest of Kendall Ridge. On a long traverse around the mountain, the path opens out in Kendall Gardens, the start of alpine color that is virtually continuous for several hiking days north. At 5⅓ miles, on a 5400-foot bump, is a happy turnaround for a day hike.

To continue involves stepping carefully along the Kendall Katwalk, blasted across a cliff in solid granite. When snowfree it's safe enough. When snowy, forget it. The mountainside moderates to heather meadows. At 6¼ miles is the 5270-foot saddle between tiny Ridge Lake and large Gravel Lake, the last permitted trail camps until Mineral Creek Park.

Overnighters based here typically day-trip to Alaska Mountain, 7¾ miles, 5745 feet, or to Huckleberry-Chikamin saddle, 10¼ miles, 5520 feet (due to ups and downs, a gross elevation gain of 1100 feet from Ridge Lake). On the way the trail swings around the basins of Alaska Lake and Joe Lake, both 1000 feet below and without recommendable sidetrails.

Rattlesnake Mountain

USGS map: North Bend

Easternmost of the Issaquah Alps, and the highest, Rattlesnake Mountain is hitched to Mt. Washington, at the Cascade front, by a terminal moraine of the Canadian glacier. The ice front was stable hereabouts quite a long while, accounting for the exceptional dimensions of the debris arc that lies across the Middle Fork and South Fork Snoqualmie valleys and also across this gap between the Cascades and Alps. Earlier the ice had crunched on through Rattlesnake Gap into the Cedar River valley, joining another arm of the Canadian glacier pushing up that valley. Rattlesnake was the only peak of the Issaquah Alps not buried, its tip riding as a rock island (nunatak) in the sea of white.

The mountain overlooks 8500 years of human prehistory, starting in hunting-fishing-berrypicking-rootdigging camps on shores of the primeval Cedar Lake, elevation 1532 feet, in the Cedar River. The Duwamish and Muckleshoot peoples came from the west and perhaps the Wenatchee from the east; the Cedar was on the Yakima Pass route across the Cascades, far more important for trade than Snoqualmie Pass because it could be traversed by horses. Raising of the lake to 1560 feet to become Chester Morse Reservoir kept campsites largely intact under the reservoir waters, available for study by archaeologists during seasonal drawdowns.

Rattlesnake Lake, formed by reservoir seepage through the moraine, drowned out Moncton, a railroaders' settlement, in 1915. Plainly discernible from Rattlesnake Ledge is a scoop in the north side of the moraine with the appearance of a grown-over gravel pit; it was here the reservoir seepage swelled into a gush one dark and stormy night of 1918, the "Boxley Burst," which took out another town, Edgewick. A third, Cedar Falls, dating from 1904, still exists, but without inhabitants since 1956, when the little hydropower plant (Seattle City Light's first) was automated. A mandatory stop on any visit to the area is the history exhibit at the Cedar Falls headquarters of Seattle City Water.

The closed-to-the-public south slopes of Rattlesnake are gentle enough to let logging roads climb to the summit ridge. The north side is steep and cliffy, and the inaccessibility has protected "long corners" of

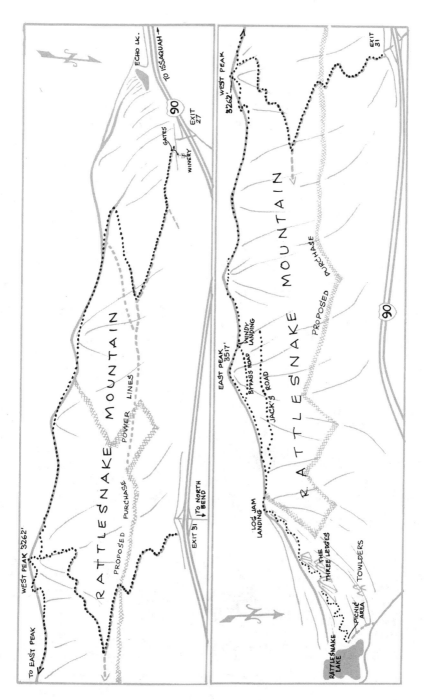

ancient forest. Lower, the forest is half-century-old second-growth and half-hour-old third-growth. At the bottom, on shores of the delta-filled great lake of glacier times, the near future may bring a 1000-acre, 2500-unit, 6500-people "Villages of North Bend."

With or without these "villages," Rattlesnake has a special spot in the hearts of urban-edge wildland walkers. The ancient forest is precious, as is the might-get-ancient forest. The upper cliffs harbor "out-of-place" subalpine plants, perhaps relicts from the Pleistocene, perhaps reestablishments by windblown or bird-carried seed from the nearby Cascades. The panoramas to Mount Si, the sweep of saltwater-ways from Olympia to the San Juan Islands, all the volcanoes the Cascades got, and more cities than the eye can wot are famous among

Town of Snoqualmie from West Peak of Rattlesnake Mountain

those who know them. Finally, the ridge is a link in the walkway from Puget Sound City to the Cascade Crest, Canada, Mexico, and Independence, Missouri.

For all that, Rattlesnake has been a sort of orphan mountain. The Issaquah Alps Trails Club long had its hands full battling "Progress" on Cougar, Squak, and Tiger Mountains. *Footsore 2,* the first edition in 1978, surveyed routes to both summits and to Rattlesnake Ledge and a north-scarp vista but had too much else on its platter to give full treatment. The 1990 Mountains to Sound March, sponsored by the Issaquah Alps Trails Club and the Snoqualmie Valley Trails Club, amounted to a public revelation. In preparation for the march and in subsequent celebration, a task force from the two clubs, the Rattlesnake Rangers, roamed and scrambled, flagging and mapping. We are proud to unveil for general inspection in these pages the World of Rattlesnake.

We have omitted two trails because as yet they don't really-truly exist, though they surely must because they will connect Rattlesnake to the other Alps. One is a low route, going from Tiger under SR 18 at the Raging River bridge and ascending Weyerhaeuser roads to the West Peak of Rattlesnake (see out-of-print *Footsore 2*). A higher and more southerly route will cross SR 18 from Tiger Mountain to Taylor Mountain via a yet-to-be-built underpass (serving both hikers and critters) near Tiger Summit (Holder Gap), pass a view of Shawn Falls, descend to cross Raging River near the site of Kerriston (such a ghost of a logging/coal-mining town it lacks even ectoplasm), and ascend Weyerhaeuser roads to the East Peak of Rattlesnake.

The publicizing energy of the Rangers aside, the addition of Rattlesnake to the realm of the public foot is being enabled by a $500,000 gift from the Bullitt Foundation to Trust for Public Land, used to purchase an option on 1800 acres of Weyerhaeuser's Northern Pacific Land Grant on the north slopes, by a state commitment of $1,000,000 toward purchase, and by an effort (apparently successful at this writing) to raise $3,500,000 more by September 1993, expiration date of the option.

Placing this handsome block of green in public ownership is crucial to the Greenway. It is hoped that other portions of the mountain remaining in hands of land-grant heirs will be managed on the pattern of Tiger Mountain State Forest, designated by the state Department of Natural Resources "a working forest in an urban environment." It is further hoped that urbanization of private lands at the mountain's base and on the adjoining North Bend Plain will duly acknowledge the spirit of the Greenway.

About that rattlesnake: A deity in the pantheon of Old Coyote? No. Hitchhiker in the bedroll of a U.S. Army soldier? No. In a hay wagon from the Kittitas Valley? No. Autumn seedpods rattling in the wind.

Rattlesnake Mountain, West Peak— From the Winery
(Map—page 161)

Round trip 11 miles, allow 8 hours
High point 3262 feet, elevation gain 2300 feet
March–November

From Grand Prospect, on the north shoulder of the West Peak of Rattlesnake Mountain, view North Bend 2700 feet below and the northern half of the world spread before you as far as the eye can see— from the Olympics to Baker to Glacier to Si to Defiance and everything in-between. Breathtaking. From Rainier Landing, on the west shoulder of the peak, see Rainier and the other half of the world. Or, from Stan's Overlook, some 1200 feet below the summit, most of the northerly view, obtained with half or less the effort. In fact, the view is partly better. This is precisely the perfect spot to grasp the incredible bulk and tallness of Si and appreciate how astoundingly it towers above the houses and pastures of North Bend.

Go off I-90 on Exit 27 and turn south on Winery Road, following signs for Snoqualmie Winery. Continue to the winery, if desired, to sample the semillon, or the early-release chardonnay, amusingly presumptuous, then walk out on the lawn. The views instantly are staggering. Easily the best family-car-accessible view in all the Greenway. A newspaper wine columnist wrote, to describe his impressions as he emerged from the tasting room, "... the late afternoon sun began to paint Mt. Si pink and then almost magenta ..."—resembling, perhaps, the "cabernet sauvignon and merlot slowly aging in the barrels." The panorama extends from the west face of Mount Si over the North Bend Plain (lakebed, once) to the village of Snoqualmie and sprawling Weyerhaeuser Mill and north to Fuller Mountain and Baker and west to the Olympics.

The hiker should not necessarily proceed as far as the winery. Instead, on Winery Road, before reaching the entrance gate to the winery (locked after hours), spot the logging-road gate on the right, partway up the hill. This is Winery Gate, often locked, elevation 960 feet. Park near here, walk through the gate, and proceed up the main logging road, Winery Road. In 0.2 mile pass a water tank on the right, a track on the left leading to the winery, and soon on the right the gated access road to the water tank. In 0.9 mile pass a lesser-traveled road branching uphill to the right. (This is Coal Mine Road, an alternative return route from West Peak; see "Powerline Prospect—Via Coal Mine Road.")

At 1.3 miles turn right steeply uphill on Plum Creek Road, newly built for the logging of Section 7 in 1990. Near the third power tower, 1800 feet, 1.8 miles from Winery Gate, turn left under the powerline and continue uphill (south). At this corner the much-lesser Power Line Road continues ahead (west) under the powerline. (Remember this intersection.) Later, on your way down from West Peak, for a pleasant alternative route home take Power Line Road 0.3 miles west to its intersection with Coal Mine Road. Turn right onto Coal Mine Road, which will take you down to Winery Road. Turn left and follow Winery Road to Winery Gate—or try the shortcut to the right opposite the water tank, which leads to the winery.

At 2 miles from Winery Gate, pass a short spur road on the right. Look sharp here to spot an orange arrow and "TR" painted on a tree at the northwest corner of the intersection. These orange spray-painted blazes (there are others ahead) mark the route of the July 1990 Mountains to Sound March through Section 7. In the spring of 1990, when we built the march trail through Section 7, it had not yet been logged. Several weeks before the march, the felling of trees destroyed a portion of our trail, which we relocated the week preceding the march. On March Day we found new road-clearing and a new gap in the trail. Confused marchers broke ranks and strayed into untrodden forest before their never-lost-for-long leaders pioneered a way through the jackstraw. Panic was avoided, barely!

Pushing on up Plum Creek Road, very shortly pass (and ignore) a spur down left. Continue straight ahead. Note the "left-trees" standing in the 1990 cut. These are prominently visible on the skyline of Rattlesnake as viewed from I-90. They were left by Plum Creek as a demonstration of its version of "new forestry." How long they will survive is a question.

At 2.1 miles pass a spur on the right, West Pond Road. Reserve this for future exploration. At 2.2 miles pass another spur on the right. This is East Pond Road, an interesting sidetrip. It heads downvalley south toward the section line, a 1992 clearcut on the hillside above and a mixed-species stand protecting Plum Pond in the swale below. Plum Pond (WL1882 on the USGS sheet) is the headwater of Skunk Creek, a

year-round stream flowing south to the Raging River. The pond is a refuge for who knows what critters—the frogs can be deafening. It is well
worth strolling through the woods to shores of the pond and farther
south to meditate in the spell of the creek. In some places the tracks of
whoever made off by the light of the moon with the old-growth cedar
here will serve as your path. A good place for a quiet lunch. It will be
instructive to observe how the pond, creek, and critters fare after the
recent logging of this quiet valley.

Proceeding again up Plum Creek Road, at 2.4 miles find a junction, the main road continuing ahead and a spur going sharp around
left up through a deep cut. Take the spur up left to an outstanding
viewpoint, Stan's Overlook (Cardtable Overlook on early Ranger
maps), elevation 2100 feet. After enjoying the splendid view, search for
orange flags and blazes in the forest uphill from the overlook if you
wish to follow the Mountains to Sound March route—the famous Orange Trail. It's still a good trail but not always easy to find here. If you
can't find it, or would rather not try, go back down, turn left, and continue up the main road.

Enjoy the views south to Taylor and west to Tiger. In ⅓ mile make
a hairpin curve to the left and ignore the spur going off right to the
south. At 3.1 miles from Winery Gate, ¼ mile above the hairpin curve,
come to a junction, 2350 feet, where a main spur goes straight ahead
and downgrade while the main road turns a square corner to the right
and proceeds upgrade. The spur going straight ahead is Quarry Road,
a not-very-interesting sidetrip. It deadends in ½ mile at a quarry with
several huge rocks poised on the edge of Owen Creek gorge, ready to
plunge down the mountain to I-90 when triggered by the next earth-
quake. Hikers below be forewarned!

This junction, Quarry Road Corner, is a key point on the trail and
should be remembered because it serves as the locating point for two
trail entrances/exits not easily found. The first of these is located 100
yards back down the main road (west) from the corner. This is where
you would have emerged onto the road had you found and followed
Orange Trail up from Stan's Overlook. On your return journey, going
down the main road, this is where you would drop down off the road to
the right to pick up Orange Trail down to Stan's Overlook. From the
edge of the road, peer down into the forest to spot orange flags marking
the trail.

The second entrance/exit to be located, Cedar Alley, lies 50 yards
up the main road (south) from the corner. Going uphill, turn off the
road to the left and walk through a gap sawn by a cedar miner in a
large log—hence, "Cedar Alley." This is the beginning of the upper sec-

tion of Orange Trail. Before describing the delights of this trail, it may be noted that another sidetrip is possible by continuing up the main road 0.4 mile to its terminal landing, 2600 feet. The view from this landing is impressive, though you will see even more of the same exposure from View Loop Road just under West Peak, which lies about 1 mile and 600 feet elevation gain farther up the trail. If you have the time and energy, West Peak via Orange Trail is a better deal. (If you walked up to this landing, did you spot the large rock perched on a stump?)

To resume, having entered at Cedar Alley, pick your way through the cedar-shake debris and head uphill toward a clump of vine maple, where you should find the flagged resumption of Orange Trail. The trail makes its way across-slope, through the 60-year-old second-growth, skirting the road and clearcut above. In ½ mile reach Blue Corner, a quarter-section corner marked by blue surveyor's blazes. The trees south and west of here were clearcut to this corner in 1992. From Blue Corner the trail angles down to the left and continues in a south-

Sword fern outlined with frost

erly direction, the open sky of the clearcut above on your right and Owen Creek below on your left. Soon cross Owen Creek, a year-round stream, the highest water found (so far) on the west ridge of Rattlesnake. (From I-90, admire Owen Falls on the lower reaches of this creek.) Next cross Sally's Swale, usually dry, and rub shoulders with several old-growth snags and BJ's "Plus Tree" (look for the yellow tags reserving this specimen for breeding better trees).

In 1 mile from Cedar Alley, emerge through Secret Entrance onto Deer Road, an old logging road. You must find this entrance on your return trip (or coming down, if you are traversing from elsewhere) so pay attention. On your return, coming down Deer Road, Secret Entrance takes off to the right just as Deer Road begins its first broad 90-degree curve to the left. The towers of West Peak are now in sight (clouds permitting) as you continue up Deer Road. In 150 yards, pass a spur going down left; you take the track up right, now somewhat overgrown. In ¼ mile merge onto a well-traveled service road (RS 100), turn left, and continue up—but first note this junction, which you must find for your return (or descent). On the way down, Deer Road branches right off the main road at the midpoint of the first sweeping curve (180 degrees left) of the main road after passing the two spurs on the right that lead up to Grand Prospect.

Coming up the main service road from Deer Road corner, in ¼ mile take the first road left to a landing and the AT&T cableway. Turn right at the AT&T concrete marker post—you should now be walking up the cableway headed straight for the mother-of-all-towers on the West Peak—red and white with numerous giant ears silently eavesdropping on the thousands of conversations that pass this way. Rather than continue up the cableway to the peak (too steep), turn left up the rock-covered road that soon crosses the cableway. This will take you at last to Grand Prospect, 3140 feet, where the view is grand indeed.

Having come this far, doubtless you will climb the final 122 feet to the summit of West Peak, 3262 feet. Do so by ascending Presidents' Staircase (stairs destroyed by motorbikers), the rock-ballasted cableway behind you leading to the easternmost high tower and thence by road to the western monster tower. No views at the very summit, so pick a route down: (1) to the east end of Grand Prospect bench, where Ridge Trail (see "Rattlesnake Mountain, West Peak—Via Ridge Trail") will take you swiftly down to Exit 31 (car there?); (2) to East Peak (see "Rattlesnake Mountain, East Peak") and then via the Ledges down to Rattlesnake Lake (car there?); (3) RS 100 or RS 240 to Rattlesnake Mainline (RSML)—8 miles by road either way—to Rattlesnake Gate (car there?); or (4) back to Winery Gate.

For route (3) or (4), or to see Rainier, leave the summit via the service road that heads southwesterly from the monster tower. In a few minutes come to Rainier Landing, from which on a good day you can see The Mountain and a whole lot more. If you turn left and go south from this landing, in 1 mile you will deadend at a landing with an even better view of Rainier, the Green River valley, and all points south and west.

To return to Winery Gate via the scenic route, turn right at Rainier Landing and proceed north and down on the service road (RS 100). For a few more years there will be fine views west and north from this loop. In ½ mile pass on the right a rock-covered road leading up to Grand Prospect and soon another road leading to the AT&T cableway concrete marker post. In ¼ mile come to Deer Road corner, with Deer Road (somewhat overgrown) heading off right halfway round the lefthand curve of the main road. If you paid attention on the way up, you should know the way back from here!

Powerline Prospect—Via Coal Mine Road
(Map—page 161)

Round trip 6 miles, allow 4 hours
High point 1800 feet, elevation gain 1150 feet
All year

A grand view from a clifftop at the end of an easy walk passing near Ralph's Coal Mine.

Drive to Winery Gate (see "Rattlesnake Mountain, West Peak—From the Winery"). Park near here.

Walk Winery Road 0.9 mile to a junction with Coal Mine Road, a less-traveled road branching uphill to the right. Proceed up Coal Mine Road 1 mile to its end at Power Line Road. A future trail will begin near this intersection. Cross Coal Creek in the ravine below, and reach Ralph's Coal Mine (tailings and artifacts) on the opposite hillside. For now, however, turn right at the intersection and continue west on Power Line Road until it ends in 1 mile at Powerline Prospect ("First Top" in *Footsore 2*), elevation 1800 feet. This is the end of the walk, a grand view and a good spot for lunch.

From this clifftop the powerline plummets to the Raging River valley below. A future trail is planned to descend from here by swinging to the left through the forest to the east side of the powerline swath, thus

Mount Si from Rattlesnake Mountain

avoiding the cliff. Once down, the trail would continue under the powerline to intersect Rattlesnake Main Line Road, turn right, and in 1 mile emerge at Rattlesnake Gate just off SR 18, where your second car would be waiting.

North Scarp Vista—Via Winery Road
(Map—page 161)

Round trip, 5 miles, allow 3 hours
High point 1600 feet, elevation gain 950 feet
All year

A Sunday stroll below the north scarp of the mountain to a panoramic viewpoint on the brink of a cliff high above the once-upon-a-time pastoral valley below.

Drive to Winery Gate (see "Rattlesnake Mountain, West Peak— From the Winery"). Park near here.

"New Forestry" (Plum Creek version) from Stan's Overlook

Walk up Winery Road, in 0.9 mile passing Coal Mine Road branching right uphill, and in 1.3 mile pass a newer road (Plum Creek Road) branching right steeply uphill. Continue ahead on Winery Road, the lesser-traveled road now.

In 2.3 miles pass a spur road on the right heading up through a clearcut to a landing; from this landing it is possible to reach West Peak via Cable Chute. As the name suggests, this is a steep route, covered with rock ballast and not recommended for the rational hiker. Hikers have been observed employing this route for a quick descent from West Peak; some have been observed taking tail-busting tumbles. Continue ahead, following the road under the powerline for the final upsy-downsy, wet-in-places track to Powerline Jumpoff ("Low Top" in *Footsore 2*), elevation 1550 feet. Here the road ends on the brink of a cliff (flowers do bloom in the spring) that provides views north to Baker and Three Fingers and Sultan and Index, up the three forks of the Snoqualmie, and up the Cedar River. And views 1000 vertical feet down to cars on I-90, cows in pastures, houses in North Bend. Above all, from this platform, just high enough to see it all but not so high it begins to lose grandeur, there is Si, the 3600 feet of rugged cliff standing hugely over the green plain.

For the adventurous, a future trail route has been flagged from Powerline Jumpoff down the ravine, crossing creeks to the landing that can be seen from the Jumpoff to the southeast. From this landing a logging road leads east to Ridge Trail Road. When this route becomes a trail, it will enable one to ascend West Peak from the winery via Ridge Trail and return via Orange Trail, a welcome variation avoiding the need to drop a car at the bottom of Ridge Trail Road (see "Rattlesnake Mountain, West Peak—Via Ridge Trail").

Rattlesnake Mountain, East Peak
(Map—page 161)

Round trip 6 miles, allow 6 hours
High point 3517 feet, elevation gain 2600 feet
March–November

The tippy-top of Rattlesnake Mountain, the East Peak, also has the biggest views in all directions, mainly because it is logged absolutely naked, no scraps of summit forest to get in the way.

Ascend Rattlesnake Ledge (to drive to the trailhead, see "Rattlesnake Ledge"). From its first knob ("Lower Ledge") dip to a saddle and find the trail skirting the cliff edge and sneaking through dense-limbed young forest dating from an old burn. Pass a second bald knob ("Middle Ledge"), another appalling cliff, and pretty much the same view as before. The trail continues up, at times in forest, at times along the brink, to the highest rock promontory ("Upper Ledge"), 2350 feet. Again a cliff and the view.

The trail reenters forest and shortly emerges to a younger stand. This section of the trail, cleared in 1990 in preparation for the Mountains to Sound March, proceeds up the ridge, keeping to the right of Seattle Watershed signs. In 0.4 mile above Upper Ledge, clamber up a slash pile to Log Jam Landing, 2830 feet. Pause here, in a field of flowers spring and summer, to enjoy the view.

To continue up, do not take the overgrown road angling to the left; this would trespass on the watershed. Instead, scramble up the cutbank to a trail flagged in 1992. In 20 minutes pick your way up a small slash pile to Jack's Road at 3020 feet, which to the right in about 1 mile deadends on the north flank of the mountain, far below East Peak.

Instead, go left 100 feet to a junction with another road, turn right and proceed uphill. In 10 minutes pass through a gravel pit, angle left, and shortly join a main road continuing northwest along the flank of the mountain below the ridge crest. In 20 minutes come to a fork. (Straight ahead lies Bypass Road, which in 1 mile reaches Windy Landing, 3400 feet. From there, in 5 minutes up Crest Trail, reach East Peak.) For a more direct route to the summit, take the left fork, the main road, which in ½ mile attains East Peak, 3517 feet, marked by a rusting airways beacon, a radio hut, and various antennae.

You are now 2600 feet above Rattlesnake Lake and 500 feet higher than Snoqualmie Pass. When the clouds clear see Rainier, the Olympics, Baker, the peaks of Snoqualmie Pass—a 360-degree view, absolutely the most enormous to be had from Rattlesnake.

East Peak of Rattlesnake Mountain

Rattlesnake Grand Traverse from Lake to Winery
(Map—page 161)

One way trip 11 miles, allow 9 hours
High points 3517 and 3262 feet, elevation gain 2600 feet
March–November

See the best of Rattlesnake Mountain—the lake, the Ledges, East Peak and West Peak—in one grand traverse—from Rattlesnake Lake to the winery. This traverse includes three routes previously described and adds a connecting link, the Crest Trail.

Start by dropping a car at Winery Gate (see "Rattlesnake Mountain, West Peak—From the Winery"). Then drive east from North Bend on Cedar Falls Way (the south half of old U.S. 10) and turn right on 436 Avenue SE (Cedar Falls Road) to Rattlesnake Lake, elevation 920 feet. Ascend Rattlesnake Mountain, East Peak (see the preceding hike).

From East Peak, 3517 feet, the Crest Trail proceeds northerly down the ridge on an overgrown four-wheel track. In 5 minutes pass Windy Landing, perched up right on the north rim of the ridge, Bypass Road heading down southeasterly.

Drop northerly off Windy Landing to again intersect Crest Trail

Powerline over west end of Rattlesnake Ridge

and continue northerly along the ridge on this track, still overgrown. In 5 minutes enter 40-foot second-growth on a better road, complete with impressive mudhole. In 10 more minutes encounter the first power pole and a spur right up to a small tin house (maybe with antenna). The surefooted may creep (cautiously) past the tin house and along a rocky spine to a slippery (beware!) rock perch—Donna's Pinnacle—a place for solitary contemplation. See Chester Morse Reservoir to the east and peer down ramparts to the north. This is no spot for children or those prone to vertigo.

Return to the main road, eventually pass a small antenna on the right, and in 2 miles from East Peak arrive at Beer Can Corner. The headwaters of the Raging River—the branch so named on the USGS sheet—lie 100 yards below, a mere trickle here. Turn right on the main-traveled road (RS 240) coming up from the left. In 10 minutes reach West Peak, 3262 feet. Complete the traverse by descending to Winery Gate (see "Rattlesnake Mountain, West Peak—From the Winery").

Rattlesnake Ledge
(Map—page 161)

Round trip 1½ miles, allow 3 hours
High point 2079 feet, elevation gain 1100 feet
February–December

In rounding the east end of Rattlesnake Mountain, the Canadian glacier ground off the tip, shaping the formidably vertical cliff that causes climbers driving along I-90 to snap their carabiners. Not only is Rattlesnake Ledge a remarkable phenomenon rewarding close inspection—the view from the top is superb. Moreover, winds sheering around the corner and sun blasting the naked rock create so severe a microclimate that flowers of the Ledge are—despite the low elevation—amazingly alpine.

Go off I-90 on Exit 32 and drive 436 Avenue SE (Cedar Falls Road) 2.7 miles to Rattlesnake Lake. On approaching the shore, turn right and follow the gravel road (if the gate is closed, on foot) 0.2 mile to the road-end, elevation 920 feet.

A person new to the trip, stretching his/her neck up at the cliff from the parking lot, may wish he/she had some carabiners to snap. However, a volunteer-built path (never really finished) ascends a route somewhat less abrupt. A concrete post at the southwest corner of the

Rattlesnake Ledge

parking area marks one of many entries to the trail, which gently climbs a short bit to an old road. Cross this road, fern-covered boulders right and left, and find the trail resumption uphill ahead.

Big stumps are passed in the second-growth, and great mossy-ferny boulders tumbled from the ice-oversteepened Ledge. The path grows steeper; several pitches of muddy rock and awkward logs are so mean that myriad detours have been built by boots (when in doubt stay left). At spots, three-point suspension is required to get up pitches of the rubbly volcanic crud, which dissuades climbers from trying the Ledge Direct. The best thing that can be said about the "trail" is that it's short. Soon comes a scramble out of the forest onto a rock nose and the first views. Thenceforth the ascent is in one or another boot-eroded gully, slippery and messy, but provided with many a thank-God shrubbery handhold.

Botanists are fascinated by the subalpine herbs and shrubs, the colors particularly gay when the phlox and lupine and penstemon and paintbrush and tiger lily and California tea are blooming. Both kinnikinnick and manzanita grow here—and also the hybrid of the two.

At ¾ mile from the parking lot is the top of the Ledge, 2079 feet. What an appalling place! Enough to give acrophobia to a mountain goat. Definitely not a spot for kiddies to toddle about—nor for teenagers to play chicken, seeing who dares make the closest approach to the brink, which for some 400 feet is vertical. A narrow cleft 20 feet deep reminds one of the huge chunks of former Ledge down in the woods.

Sit a while on the north side of the Ledge and look out to I-90 and North Bend and gigantic Si. Move to the east brink and look up the Middle Fork to Russian Buttes and Garfield, up the South Fork past the portal peaks of Mailbox/Garcia and Washington, and dizzily down down to Rattlesnake Lake and the tidy (no residents) community of Cedar Falls and up the Cedar River to Chester Morse Reservoir. Note the "gravel cirque" (now aldery) in the moraine. This is the site of the Boxley Burst, which occurred in 1918 when Seattle filled the reservoir behind its Masonry Dam to the top and the water burst through the moraine, washing 2,000,000 cubic yards of glacial drift down Boxley Creek, obliterating dozens of homes—the entire town of Edgewick. Move to the south side and look out the Cedar to MacDonald and Enumclaw.

The original route to the Ledge beat through the woods from Cedar Falls Road, climbed a fence (easy, but $25 fine if you got caught), and scrambled a rockslide gully to the saddle immediately west of the Lower Ledge. The climbers in one party chanced on a serendipity, the "Rattlesnake Towlders" (tower + boulder = "towlder," a portmanteau word). These were not erratics dropped by the glacier but chunks of Rattlesnake Ledge. They gave splendid sport, the best bouldering in Western Washington outside the Devils Garden of Fire Mountain; the lurking menace of the Sanitary Patrolman added spice. The end of the affair was this surveyor's catastrophic $100 ascent of the Ledge (adjusted for inflation, close to $500 in 1990s money). In the late 1980s this surveyor, mourning his share of the fine, a heavy blow in the poverty year of 1961, returned to search for the scene. A road built for unknown purposes now crossed the route. To the left was the new trail. He turned right—and rediscovered the Towlders! In the 1950s their clean faces and arêtes stood high above shrubby Douglas firs. Now, dimly visible in the deep shade of those firs now almost ready for another clearcutting, they were mossy, leaf-cluttered, dirty. The good news is their challenge now is free of financial risk. Climbers should bring rakes and brooms and wire brushes.

Rattlesnake Mountain, West Peak— Via Ridge Trail
(Map—page 161)

Round trip 6 miles, allow 6 hours
High point 3262 feet, elevation gain 2800 feet
March–November

Attain the western summit and its superb views after an aerobic climb up the shortest (and steepest) path to the top. Definitely not for couch potatoes, children, and beginners, and distinctly not yet a trail, Ridge Trail-to-be follows the route of the proposed tramway from North Bend to the revolving restaurant and alpine center proposed on the West Peak.

Go off I-90 on Exit 31 and turn south, then east, to the entrance to Forster Woods. Park here or near, elevation 450 feet.

Enter Forster Woods, turn right, then left (Hemlock Avenue SW), and walk south through the development and up a logging road toward the mountain. Pass a rusting gate, a spur on the right, and in 0.8 mile another spur on the right. (This spur ascends to the landing from which a future trail route has been flagged down through the ravine and up to Powerline Jumpoff.)

In 1 mile pass under the powerline and in 2 miles pass a spur on the right, to a landing below. Soon after, pause at a corner with a view,

West Peak of Rattlesnake Mountain

the last until Grand Prospect. In 2.5 miles reach the road-end landing, 2000 feet, and the beginning of the Ridge Trail-to-be, which heads off left up the ridge from the landing. Follow orange flags (if any remain) as the ill-defined path snakes steeply up, ascending over 1100 feet in ½ mile. Stay on the ridge crest to avoid dangerous cliffs on the left (southeast) and more cliffs on the right (northwest) at the edge of the clearcut ravine below. At the end of an exhilarating climb emerge from forest at the east end of Grand Prospect, a quarry bench, 3140 feet. Enjoy the superb view and then proceed up Presidents' Staircase to West Peak, 3262 feet, and the jungle of towers.

Cedar River Watershed

Thoughtful members of the pedestrian community are content, indeed pleased, to be excluded from free access to the 90,500-acre Cedar River Watershed. Forget for the moment that the 143 square miles of the river's drainage basin supply 1.2 million residents of Puget Sound City 108 million gallons a day of the purest water any big city could wish. The U.S. Forest Service, proponent of multiple-use, insists the watershed could be opened wide to the public and the purity maintained by filtration. Hunters get twitchy trigger fingers thinking of the elk herd, one of the largest in the Northwest, and camp for days and nights on Taylor Mountain waiting for beasts to jump the fence into the free-fire zone.

Hikers, however, support limited-use. They cheer the decision by the Seattle City Council to restrict future logging to about 400 acres of second-growth a year, dedicating all the revenue to habitat acquisition, and to preserve untouched the 3000 acres of ancient forest it currently owns—and all that to be newly acquired. (In October 1992 the Forest Service was directed by Congress to exchange the 21,000 acres it presently manages, thus eventually placing the entire watershed in Seattle care.)

Not for a public park. For water purity? Yes. For gene-pool preserves? Yes. But also for a serendipity—a refuge safeguarding the largest wildlife population so close to any large city of the planet.

Just about every animal native to the region is domiciled: elk (more than 600) and black bear and bobcat and lynx and some 15 resident cougar, as many deer as the cats need for supper, a few mountain goats, coyotes and skunks-porcupine-weasels-raccoons-beavers-aplodontia-moles-voles-shrews-rats-mice. They move freely out of the watershed sanctuary to Rattlesnake and Taylor, thence to Tiger, Squak, and Cougar, and thence to the outer neighborhoods of Puget Sound City. The watershed/Issaquah Alps/Greenway serve to constantly replenish near-urban populations.

Of six pairs of common loons known to nest in Washington in 1989, three were in the watershed, and an osprey pair, too. Harlequin ducks, common mergansers, swans, and other waterfowl nest or winter, as do a circus of raptors and corvids and dickybirds. The ancient forests are home to spotted, great-horned, and pygmy owls and pileated and hairy

Rattlesnake Lake and Cedar River Watershed

woodpeckers, and the waters to sandpipers and dippers. Golden eagles patrol the high ridges and bald eagles fish the streams. Tailed frogs, Pacific giant salamanders....

To a society that increasingly prizes wildlife habitat in close proximity to people habitat, the Cedar River Watershed is a treasure house whose riches are more than water. At least one mountain sheep has been sighted. Wolves have been reported. Someday the grizzly may be allowed to return.

The public is not excluded. Hikers can look down into the Cedar River Watershed from trails on Taylor and Rattlesnake and Cedar Butte and Washington and McClellan Butte; management of certain watershed-edge sites is being reviewed to accommodate edge-trails wherever compatible with water quality. School classes and groups of other wildlife lovers are conducted on guided tours into the sanctuary. For information call (206) 888-1507.

From the North Bend Plain to the Cascade Crest: The South Ridge

USGS map: North Bend
Green Trails maps: Bandera, Snoqualmie Pass

The South Ridge Trail is the longest of the proposed high lines from lowlands to Cascades. In effect it starts in the heart of Puget Sound City, climbing from shores of Lake Washington to the Issaquah Alps, traversing Cougar and Squak and Tiger and Taylor to Rattle-

Christmas Lake

snake. Rattlesnake Gap is bridged by the moraine of the Canadian glacier, hitching the Alps to the Cascade front at Cedar Butte and Mount Washington, where the South Ridge proper begins.

Footsore 1 treats the walking from Elliott Bay to Tiger Mountain, and a preceding section of this book the traverse of Rattlesnake Mountain. The route in hand is from Cedar Butte to Washington to McClellan Butte to Kent to Gardner and the Pacific Crest National Scenic Trail. Turn left for Canada, right for Mexico.

Most likely to be completed first is the stretch east from McClellan Butte. For a decade the U.S. Forest Service has been scouting the terrain, joined recently by volunteers from the Washington Trails Association. The plan is to connect the existing McClellan Butte trail to the abandoned and mostly clearcut Gardner Mountain trail, relocating on a line compatible with the Cedar River Watershed, proceeding perhaps over Abiel Peak to the Cascade Crest at Tinkham Peak or Silver Peak. The concept embodies a loop combining Ridge Trail and Iron Horse Trail, the McClellan Butte trail serving as the link on the west, a new trail to be built as the eastern link, likely in or near Humpback Creek.

The South Ridge will have more than one trail. The system will include foot-only trails, foot/horse trails, and fat-tire bikeways. Certain of the logging roads perhaps can be kept sufficiently open for street-legal motorcycles and 4 x 4 playcars. A few might be maintained to permit Sunday-Drive family cars to picnic at high viewpoints. Assuredly, recreation is replacing logging as the central industry hereabouts; so total has been the clearcutting, to elevations and slopes and soils so impossible for tree-farming, that the clearcutters would like to go away quietly, get quickly out of the accusing public eye. They wish to exchange their stumps for public trees elsewhere, which they can clearcut demurely out of the spotlight.

West from McClellan Butte the ownership is non-federal; after land exchanges the manager will be, in the main if not entirely, the state Department of Natural Resources, which already has acquired substantial tracts near Mount Washington. The prospect of linking the McClellan Butte trail to Cedar-Washington urges on bands of volunteers, and the distance is so short that no heroic effort will be required.

The two parallel paths, South Ridge Trail and Iron Horse Trail, will attract the long-leggity walkers bent on Canada, Mexico, or Independence, Missouri. The day-hiker and backpacker already enjoy trails from Snoqualmie Valley to lakes and peaks and backcountry camps. There will be more. Must be more. The Alpine Lakes Wilderness needs help.

Iron Horse Trail
(Map—page 185)

One way from Cedar Falls Junction 18 miles
High point 2400 feet, elevation gain 1500 feet
Western end, all year; eastern end, March–November

In 1981 the State of Washington acquired 213 miles, from Easton to Idaho, of the defunct Milwaukee Railroad and placed them in management of the Department of Natural Resources. In 1984 the legislature transferred the western 25 miles to a new Iron Horse State Park. In 1988 State Parks entered into a lease-purchase agreement with Burlington-Northern Railroad for the deeded and non-reversionary property along the 36.57 miles of right-of-way between Cabin Creek and Cedar Falls acquired by Burlington-Northern when Milwaukee went belly-up and which it was now itself abandoning. The hiker/ horserider community greeted with elation the resulting Iron Horse Trail, a non-motorized way from the edge of the lowland at Cedar Falls to (or rather, under) the Cascade Crest.

Elation quieted in December 1991 when it was revealed that on 14 of the 21 miles east from Cedar Falls the old powerline along the trail was to be replaced by a new 230kw line and its service road. Hikers experienced in walking powerlines say, "On a rainy day your umbrella buzzes. You feel your bones buzzing, too. Your brain acts electrified. You imagine you're a character in science fiction. Clear days are worse. Knowing the stuff is there but not being able to hear it is even scarier." A hiker who loved walking the rail grade before Puget Power cut a 40-foot swath of forest beside the new powerline says, "The trail no longer gives a sense of walking through a woodland tunnel. The swath destroys the sense of solitude." The *Seattle Times* editorialized, "The Mountains to Sound Greenway idea has captured the fancy of the entire region.... But surely, 14 miles of trail under unsightly, buzzing high-voltage lines is not what Greenway visionaries had in mind."

Puget Power is in the business of bringing power to the people at the lowest possible cost, and that is good. It would be nice, though, if the people were given a voice in deciding among alternative ways to bring them the power. Large corporations dislike the inconvenience of conversing with people. In this case Puget Power seems to have belatedly listened to the people—or at least, the *Seattle Times*. A proposition put forth by the Snoqualmie Valley Trails Club is (perhaps) under consideration: Relocating as much as possible of the trail on the former powerline route, now abandoned, and letting the trees there grow up, a

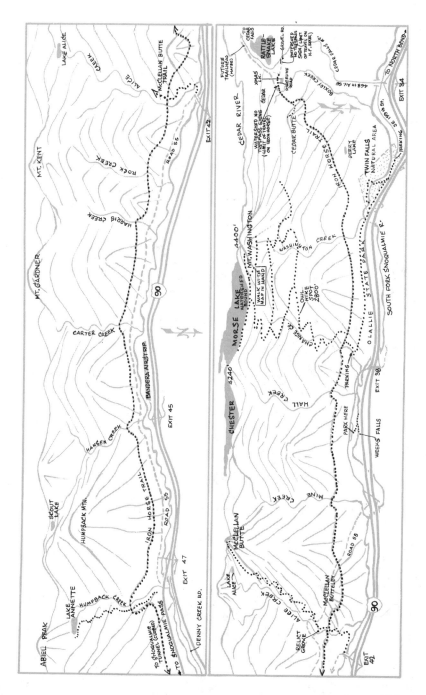

185

Rattlesnake Ledge and East Peak of Rattlesnake Mountain from Iron Horse Trail

new woodland tunnel. No service road. No buzzing.

To give the 40-foot swath its due, the views are better from a clearcut than a tunnel. Some 14 of the 21 miles now have an uninterrupted panorama from Si to Mailbox to Granite and to the busy-ness in the valley below. The scenic climaxes are the creeks. Those crossed near grade on fills invite the picnic basket to the waterfalls. Those that cross high in the air offer exhilarating (to the acrophobe, terrifying) trestles. The 21 miles feature these named creeks: Washington, Change, Hall, Wood, Mine, Alice, Rock, Harris, Carter, Hansen, Humpback, Olallie, and Rockdale, averaging out to a major creek every 2 miles. Numberless nameless babbles and trickles water the intervals; in springtime, multiply the numberless by a score, promote trickles to snowmelt flushes.

Iron Horse Trail will be less used by hikers than service trucks, fat-tire bicycles, and horses. However, in proper season on proper days (a Tuesday morning in February during a snowstorm is suggested) a person will find more or less pleasure in walking shorter or longer stretches of the trail from various accesses.

Among the most popular will be the west end. Go off I-90 on Exit 32, turn south on 436 Avenue SE (Cedar Falls Road) toward (but not *to*) Rattlesnake Lake, elevation 970 feet.

Eventually, when State Parks tidies up the trail and Seattle City Water completes its recreation plan, Iron Horse Trail will start at Rattlesnake Lake. Until then, "No Trespassing" signs must be obeyed. For now, to begin on the trail, about ½ mile past Wilderness Rim and ¼ mile short of the lake, turn off left on a wide gravel road. Park at the first sharp bend, where the barbed wire fence on concrete posts marks the watershed boundary. The trail follows the fence, skirting Christmas Lake to the access road built for the new Puget powerline. Follow this up to the old Milwaukee mainline, now Iron Horse Trail, which is reached about 1 mile east of the to-be trailhead near Cedar Falls junction and Rattlesnake Lake.

The trail crosses Boxley Creek, rounds the slopes of Cedar Butte (see "Cedar Butte"), and reaches the Cascade front at Mount Washington. A popular day-hike destination is the trestle over the waterfalls of

Snoqualmie Pass tunnel

Washington Creek, 1100 feet, 2 miles from Boxley Creek (3 miles from the Cedar Falls junction trailhead of the future).

Another popular access is Olallie State Park (see "Olallie State Park"), from the upper Twin Falls trailhead, elevation 1200 feet. The rail grade is intersected in a few yards. Walk west a scant 1 mile to the Washington Creek trestle. Walk east to Change Creek and then Hall Creek—but where's the Hall Creek trestle? A blowout flood from skinned mountainsides flushed it to the river. A rude ¼-mile path descends into the gulch and climbs back to grade. Onward, then, to Mine Creek, Wood Creek, and, at 9 miles from Boxley Creek, Alice Creek at 1800 feet.

The lower part of the McClellan Butte trail (see "McClellan Butte"; trailhead elevation 1580 feet) to Relict Grove is a longer access but more interesting than the Puget Power service road. The walk west from the intersection, 1760 feet, around the snub nose of McClellan Buttelet, used to be a fond choice. The walk east crosses Alice, Rock, and Harris Creeks (1900 feet) in a scant 2 miles, a lot of water excitement. In another 5 miles (passing Carter and Hanson Creeks and going through a snowshed) is Humpback Creek.

The Annette Lake trail (see "Annette Lake") starts from a trailhead at 2000 feet and parallels Humpback Creek to the rail grade in ¾ mile, 2400 feet. A two-car shuttle combines the McClellan Butte trailhead and the Annette Lake trailhead in a one-way hike of some 10 miles.

The first 1½ miles east from Humpback Creek pass Olallie Creek, the site of the old Rockdale Station, from which The Mountaineers' trail ascended to Lodge Lake (see "Lodge Lake"), and come to the west portal of the tunnel. The sky reappears 2¼ miles east at Hyak. The tunnel is not open to the public at present, but an over-the-top route on existing trails can be walked and ultimately will be formalized.

Cedar Butte
(Map—page 185)

Round trip 3 miles, allow 2 hours
High point 1840 feet, elevation gain 800 feet
All year

In the late 1930s, when Puget Sound climbers were taking a great leap upward, the monthly bulletin of The Mountaineers published lists of members' feats. It was there that the club community first learned about the conquests of Forbidden, Formidable, Challenger, Terror, Triumph, and Despair. Among the listings one month was "Herpicide Spire." The close-knit company of first-ascenders didn't know what or where that was. Discovering it was the renamed "Old Baldy" and that the reported first ascent by Mountaineers had been preceded by any number of logger and hunter ascents, the established heroes were not amused.

In the 1950s the old scandal came to the ears of a new group of irreverent alpinists. They were bonded by an agreement that the mountain snows of spring were good for glissading, those of summer for cooling drinks, and those of fall for esthetic photographs; the winter abundance, on the other hand, was a confounded nuisance. Skiing, to them, was loudspeaker-bellowed yodeling records and fannies being waggled for the delectation of the various sexes, a style later adopted by bicyclists. Their fastidious winters were devoted to the quest for (as

Grouse Ridge and Mailbox Peak from Cedar Butte

described in *The Mountaineer*) "Things To Climb When Mountains
Aren't Worth It." Aside from University of Washington buildings, their
favorites were "blobs."

The Issaquah Blobs were transformed for political purposes in
1976 into the Issaquah Alps. The North Bend Blobs remain just that.
Blobber Tom Miller, who invented Mountaineer guidebooks, bought
war-surplus U.S. Army blanket pins (1 cent apiece), burned on the
words, "BLOB PEAK PIN," and awarded them to victorious climbers. More
than a badge of honor on the order of the Snoqualmie Peaks and Six
Major Peaks Pins, the Blob Peak Pin could be employed to hold up
pants and field-repair Trapper Nelsons. The honor was not minor.
Little Si lacked a summit trail, and when the moss was soaked by rain,
as it was all fall and winter and spring and much of summer, the slabs
would have got the wind up in Rebuffat. Neither did Fuller Mountain
have a trail, and though the rockslide gully was easy enough, to get
there required the crossing of a swamp in whose depths could be seen
gray faces and empty eyes of failed adventurers. No more than a half-
dozen Blob Peak Pins ever were awarded; one went to Pete Schoening,
who is known also for trips to the Karakoram and Antarctica, though
he got no pins there. Awards would have been more plentiful had not
the location of the third blob been a closely held secret. Herpicide Spire
was not to be found on any map, and few Mountaineers who saw Cedar
Butte while driving by North Bend recognized it as the mythic Third Blob.

In the 1980s a generation of newcomers made the ascent a fad and
now romp up and down and around, 101 Essentials in their rucksacks
and carrot sticks in their teeth and no notion in their heads of where
they are, historically. These new walkers do not risk being captured on
the wrong side of the fence by a City of Seattle Sanitary Patrolman and
getting nailed for $25 a customer (big dollars those were, for a climber
supporting a family on $200 a month).

Go off I-90 on Exit 32, turn south on 436 Avenue SE (Cedar Falls
Road) and drive toward Rattlesnake Lake, elevation 970 feet. But until
Seattle City Water implements plans-in-progress, do not drive all the
way. Start from the temporary trailhead for Iron Horse Trail (described in preceding hike). Turn left on the old rail grade and in ¼ mile
cross Boxley Creek. About 175 yards past the bridge, where the grade
starts a curve, find the start of the Cedar Butte trail off to the right,
elevation 1080 feet.

Partway up the Butte cross an old logging railroad grade; a bit farther cross it again. From this second crossing the established (boring)
trail proceeds straight up the Butte. A more interesting route turns
right on the grade to the precipice of the Blowout, where City Water

reservoir water leaked through the moraine, then in 1918 gushed through and washed away the hamlet of Edgewick. Follow the Blowout around to the left, watching for orange-and-black ribbons near the ridge top; these mark the new trail, which leads back to the old trail. The final third is pretty steep; walk carefully the short bit to the summit, 1880 feet. Stay clear of brush, which masks a dangerous cliff brink on the north. Find the benchmark stamped, "1937 CEDER BUTT."

Immediately to the east lifts Mount Washington, the Cascade front. Close west is Rattlesnake Ledge, terminus of the Issaquah Alps. North across the North Bend Plain stands Mount Si. South is the Cedar River valley, featuring the Masonry Pool, Chester Morse Reservoir (the drowned Cedar Lake), and legendary Little Mountain, which is reputed never to have been climbed except by loggers.

It is expected that in the future this surveyor will tell of a trail, now being scouted, from Cedar Butte to Mount Washington.

Olallie State Park
(Map—page 185)

The geological story: The glacier descending the Middle Fork Snoqualmie was larger and more powerful than that down the South Fork. The smaller glacier couldn't cut as deep as the larger and in melting away left a "hanging trough." When the river broke through the huge moraine (Grouse Ridge) of the subsequent Canadian ice sheet, it quickly reached hard rock, forming "Upper Snoqualmie Falls" or "Twin Falls."

The human history: Puget Power, during the period when it was seeking to lock up hydropower sources in Western Washington (in the 1920s it sought state legislation to forbid public generation and distribution of electricity), bought the land adjoining Twin Falls. In the era when nuclear appeared to be the power of the future, Twin Falls was too piddling to be of interest and the land was sold to State Parks, which commenced a long period of benign neglect—entirely proper to an area officially designated Twin Falls Natural Area. When nuclear power fizzled and the nation began scrambling for energy, Congress passed what is commonly known as the "Small Hydro Act." The admirable expectation was to squeeze "low head" kilowatts out of, say, irrigation canals, city water reservoirs, and sewer discharges. The result was a "Small Hydro Rush," not to the innocuous spots expected but to "high head" sites in the nation's mountains. Congress offered such incentives that investments were no-risk, the profits not enormous but guaranteed.

We quote from page 123 of *Trips and Trails* (Seattle: The Mountaineers, 1986), by our fellow surveyor, E. M. Sterling:

> *Sorry, too late now to see the pristine Twin Falls plunging full and free.... Water that once foamed unchecked over the spectacular falls is now being diverted through a private power plant.*
>
> *In a nutshell, the Washington State Parks Commission allowed a private company, South Fork Resources, Inc., to divert the water through tunnels around the falls to generate electricity for Puget Sound Power and Light....*
>
> *From the beginning, the parks commission stood aside while the private firm obtained a license from the Federal Energy Regulating Commission ... despite findings by the Northwest Power Planning Council that there was no predictable need for electricity from the waterfall at all....*

Twin Falls Natural Area

Round trip to bridge 2.6 miles, allow 2 hours
High point 1000 feet, elevation gain 500 feet
All year

Olallie State Park is in two parts. Twin Falls Natural Area is famed for the most scenic and toddler-friendliest path in all the Greenway, the perfect year-round spot to show visitors from afar a typical Northwest magnificence of forests and waters. The trail passes through moss-and-fern-covered trees, a cathedral of ancient forest beside a murmuring river, then ascends to a thundering climax at a footbridge spanning canyon and falls. These recreation amenities were the "amelioration" the hydro developers were required to provide in exchange for their free use of public waters.

Go off I-90 on Exit 34, signed "Edgewick Road." From the interchange turn right (south) on 468 Avenue 0.5 mile. Just before the river crossing, turn left on SE 159 Street, signed "Twin Falls State Park." In 0.5 mile are the road-end parking area, toilets, and trailhead, elevation 600 feet.

The trail start is a toddler's delight, through sky gardens of moss in groves of vine maple, superb old second-growth, and fern-carpeted forest and by riverbars that invite picnicking, wading, and watching dippers and kingfishers. At ½ mile is Twin Falls Overlook, a bench to

Lower Twin Falls from unmarked side trail

sit on, and a postcard view of the falls. The trail winds on down through a grove of even-bigger trees—don't miss the 8-foot-diameter spruce on the left and the 9-foot-diameter fir on the right.

From this grove the way climbs within earshot of trucks on I-90 to meet the stairway down to Lower Falls Overlook, an aerial perch with a dramatic view. A few more minutes up the trail is *the bridge!* Stand in midspan a hundred feet above the pools between upper and lower falls. Feel the earth tremble. Wonder how the two huge laminated wooden beams were placed here. (Answer: very carefully, by helicopter.)

A hundred yards up from the bridge is Upper Falls Overlook, a good turnaround. To go onward is to soon reach Iron Horse Trail; turn left and watch for the path angling down to the Exit 38 trailhead (see "Weeks Falls").

The hydroelectric development at Twin Falls is completely underground, invisible to the walker's eye, an apparent model of non-harmful "small hydro." However, though terms of the permit require some water always to be held from diversion into the underground pipe, in the months after the melting of winter snows the spectacle is greatly diminished from old. A visit is best timed for periods when the river carries more water than South Fork can put to work. In floodtime the human shrieks are lost in the Judgment Day of pounding waters, splintering logs, and swirling spray.

Weeks Falls

Round trip to falls overlook 1 mile, allow 1 hour
High point 1200 feet, no elevation gain
All year

The Weeks Falls section of Olallie State Park features a readily accessible overlook of a minor falls and a trail to points of historic interest.

Go off I-90 at the west end of Exit 38 and turn right, over the river. To the right is the entrance to the upper Twin Falls parking area and trailhead. Continue on the main road (old U.S. 10) 0.8 mile to the Weeks Falls access road and parking area, on the left by the house, elevation 1200 feet.

Explore the trail upstream beside the river through a forest of cedar, hemlock, and fir. Look for a relict section of Sunset Highway as it heads for a decaying bridge abutment.

Alternatively, continue past the house on the Weeks Falls access road to the turnaround at the end. Toilets here, a paved walk past the

Weeks Falls, Olallie State Park

hydroelectric project to the falls overlook, and an interpretive sign explaining the whole business. Park wherever and explore the rest of the trails downstream from the project. Don't miss the historic section of puncheon road (signed) dating from the early 1890s, abandoned in 1915 upon completion of the original Sunset Highway. Also, enjoy wading the river or skipping a few stones from one of the several access points along the riverside trail.

Mount Washington
(Map—page 185)

The surveyor first began eyeing this portal peak in the 1960s. By 1970 he had spotted the correct logging road taking off from U.S. 10, but whenever he tried to scoot his beetle into the slot a monster truck was riding his rear bumper. He gave up on that, found a parkable highway shoulder farther east, beat his way up the brush to the railroad tracks, and walked west to a dead stop at a long and giddy trestle. In those years the trains were still running and he knew that if he were out in the middle and heard diesels throbbing he would expire on the spot without the formality of plummeting into the canyon.

Though other *Footsore* problems took his attention, the unfinished business always was on his mind. What joy, then, to read a route description by Jim and Ginny Evans in the September 1985 *Signpost Magazine*. Away he went. Not to the summit; winter was coming on and his Shelties were shivering in the belly-deep (theirs) snow. But to the Owl Hike Spot.

Owl Hike Spot

Round trip to Owl Hike Spot 4 miles, allow 4 hours
High point 2800 feet, elevation gain 1600 feet
March–November

Go off I-90 on the west end of Exit 38, turn right over the river, and park either on the shoulder of old U.S. 10, now a recreation road, or, if the state park gate is open, in the lot a short bit up a gravel lane to the right, elevation 1200 feet.

Ascend the lane to the old rail grade, now Iron Horse Trail, and walk west some 500 feet. Green paint and varicolored ribbons mark the trailhead on the left.

The well-maintained path (by several distinct companies of assorted volunteers) follows what the old map calls "jeep trail." Actually it's a gypo logging road of the 1950s or so. In mind's eye see Dirty Harry's decrepit truck, the outside edge overhanging a cliff, Harry at the wheel singing "Nearer My God to Thee." A clever little road-trail it is, picking a devious and ingenious way under and over and between cliffs, gaining elevation steadily and steeply, switchbacking east three times and west three times, finally traversing westward toward the objective. The way is largely in young alder but partly in virgin hemlock with several groves of ancient Douglas fir snagtops (beware of the golden eagles). The cliffs are great fun, plummeting below, beetling above—some overhanging, forming impressive caves (beware of the jaws that bite, the claws that scratch). Springs gush from crevices and nourish hangings of maidenhair fern and saxifrages. In season the icicles are dazzling.

Windows open in the forest, first down to the freeway and across to Grouse Ridge, Mailbox/Garcia, and Dirty Harry's Country, then up the Middle Fork from Si to Bessemer. Finally, about 2 miles from the

Frozen waterfall on trail to Owl Hike Spot

trailhead, the little old road rounds a cliff corner into the broad valley of Washington Creek. Here, at 2800 feet, is the famous Owl Hike Spot, so called because since 1959 (why didn't anybody tell the surveyor?) it has been a favorite evening hike of The Mountaineers, who cook a picnic supper, watch the sunset, and descend by flashlight. The panorama is a three-star gasper, from Rattlesnake over the North Bend lakebed (South and Middle forks meandering along either side, freeway slicing through the middle, towns of North Bend and Snoqualmie sprawling) to Little Si and Big Si and Teneriffe, out the Snoqualmie Falls notch to lowlands and Olympics—and straight down precipices to the gorge of Twin Falls.

The Summit

Round trip 12 miles, allow 8 hours
High point 4400 feet, elevation gain 3400 feet
May–October

Since the first report by the Evanses, *Signpost Magazine* has been full of Washington. Everybody has an opinion. The surveyor hasn't wanted to get involved. According to Mick Campbell (February 26, 1991),

At the Owl Hike Spot the trail turns south into the valley between Washington and Point 4360, which is 0.8 mile east–northeast of the summit. Descending slightly, then rising gradually, the trail crosses the creek, climbs the west side of the valley, descends again a bit, and crosses the creek once more. (Shortly before the first crossing, flags up a very steep bank may have denoted the shortcut described by the Evanses; that way did not look inviting so we stuck to Penberthy's trail.)

Steep gravelly switchbacks lead to a confluence of logging roads at 3 miles, 3400 feet. These are well-shown on the Green Trails map. Ironically, the proper road is the one heading north-northeast, directly away from the summit of Washington. Follow this up and up to the north and east side of Point 4360. The road then passes south across the "Great Wall" between your creek to the west and Change Creek to the east and ascends to the ridge north of Chester Morse Reservoir. Turn right and follow the road west, then northwest to a cat track at 4100 feet which leads to the summit.

The pioneers are not a company of a single mind and some are solitary eccentrics. Their tastes in ribbon color differ but all love to scatter it about. With ribbonry they debate the merits of their inventions in a maze of clearcut cat tracks. The judgment by hikers who are not party to the debate is that at best the way is trial-and-error. They advise:

"Walk with Green Trails map in hand, always be prepared to retreat and try something else."

Note: Other companies of pioneers are scouting from Cedar Butte up the west escarpment of Washington.

McClellan Butte
(Map—page 185)

The appearance of the McClellan Butte from I-90 is formidable and the final short scramble to the summit is truly life-threatening. Furthermore, until early or middle July there may be crossings of steep snow that ought to stop hikers but don't always. However, in late summer the trail can be ascended safely to panoramas west over lowlands to Seattle, Puget Sound, and the Olympics, south over moth-eaten ridges to Rainier, and east over stark clearcuts to Snoqualmie Pass. But that's the long of it; this is two trips in one, and the short of it is something completely different, culminating in the rare (hereabouts) ancient forest of Relict Grove.

Relict Grove

Round trip 2 miles, allow 2 hours
High point 2200 feet, elevation gain 700 feet
March–November

Go off I-90 on Exit 43, signed "Tinkham Road," and turn right across the South Fork Snoqualmie to the trailhead, elevation 1500 feet.

The way begins at the site of historic Camp Mason, once the last outpost of civilization east of North Bend, and wanders through mossy forest grown up since the 1920s; note stumps of trees that were centuries old when cut and rotting logs centuries older that were too monstrous to haul to the mill. Beyond a delicious little picnic creek barely minutes from the car, even as a toddler goes, the path follows the wire-wrapped wooden pipeline (long-ago Camp Mason water supply) to Alice Creek. Crossing cataracts on a bridge, the trail begins to climb. Exits from mossy woods to a powerline swath. Reenters. Passes a waterfall gushing from a railroad culvert, intersects the grade of the temporary rail line built early in the century and soon abandoned; a few steps left are decrepit remains of the trestle over Alice Creek.

A few steps higher is the newer rail grade, now also abandoned and become Iron Horse Trail. The summit trail enters young forest grown up since a 1960s clearcut and parallels the gorge of Alice Creek to the ancient trees of Relict Grove. How has it survived amid universal down-to-the-last-bush clearcutting? A patented mining claim whose heirs are so distant in time from their ancestors and so residentially obscure to famished log-exporters they haven't got around to turning a profit? Yet? Is it conceivable that some property owner, somewhere, has a social-ecological conscience?

Relict Grove is (if it's still there) a satisfying turnabout. A lot of action for so short a walk. The portable artifacts of the mine have vanished but heavy chunks of iron have defied scavengers. Just above the grove at 2200 feet, 1 mile from the trailhead, is what used to be and to some extent still is a mainline log-haul road.

The Summit

Round trip from lower trailhead 9 miles, allow 8 hours
High point 5162 feet, elevation gain 3700 feet
July–October

Now, about that mainline. It used to be gated at the highway and thus a fine footroad; being closed to public machines put the summit of the Butte that much deeper in trail country. It still can be. Many folks will take the cheating shortcut; bad news. The good news is that the opening of the road makes an exciting addition to the Sunday Drive.

For Sunday Drivers (devout hikers, shut your eyes), go off I-90 on the west entry to Exit 38 and drive the rest-and-recreation road (old U.S. 10) to the east entry to Exit 38. Turn right onto good gravel road No. 55, which in some 10 miles comes to the sideroad entry from Exit 47, whose interchange leads across I-90 to Denny Creek Road and thence to Snoqualmie Pass. The Sunday Drive therefore is not a far-fetched dream: it presently exists from Exit 38 to the pass and only needs some work west of Grouse Ridge to take the family to North Bend, the whole way free and innocent of freeway.

At a scant 3 miles east from the R&R highway on road No. 55 is the summit trail, 2200 feet. The way becomes steadily steep, going by a sometime spring in a cool grove of large trees, then switchbacking up the wooded north face of the Butte. At about 2½ miles the trail rounds the east side of the Butte and crosses an avalanche gully with a treacherous snowbank that usually lasts into July. From here, with numerous switchbacks, the way sidehills below cliffs in occasional views, attaining the south ridge of the peak at 3¼ miles, 4500 feet. The trail

South Fork Snoqualmie River valley from McClellan Butte

follows the crest a short bit, looking down into Seattle's Cedar River Watershed, rounds the east side of the mountain, drops 100 feet to a small pond, and climbs again, passing mining garbage to a magnificent viewpoint on the ridge crest about 100 vertical feet from the summit.

The majority of hikers are content with the ridge-top view and leave the summit for experienced mountaineers; the rocks are slippery when wet and the exposure is sufficient to be fatal.

Annette Lake
(Map—page 185)

Round trip 7¼ miles, allow 4 hours
High point 3600 feet, elevation gain 1400 feet
June–November

A super-popular subalpine lakelet below cliffs and talus of Abiel Peak, ringed by open forest and masses of humanity, much of it very young. For quiet walking try early summer or late fall in the middle of the week in a storm.

Go off I-90 on Exit 47 and turn right 0.1 mile, then left on road No. 55 for 0.6 mile to the parking lot, elevation 2200 feet.

The way starts in an old clearcut, crosses Humpback Creek, and in 1 mile passes under a powerline and enters forest. At 1¼ miles, 2400 feet, cross Iron Horse Trail.

Now comes the hard part, switchbacking steeply upward in nice old forest on the slopes of Silver Peak, occasional talus openings giving

Annette Lake

looks over the valley to Humpback Mountain. After gaining 1200 feet in 1½ miles, at the 3600-foot level the way flattens and goes along a final mile of minor ups and downs to the lake outlet, 3 miles, 3600 feet.

Wander along the east shore for picnic spots with views of small cliffs and waterfalls.

Folks planning to camp do well to call the Forest Service beforehand to learn if and when and where and how they can; the lake is so mobbed that great care is being taken to avoid making it a muddy-dusty slum.

Cold Creek–Silver Peak Loop
(Map—page 203)

Loop trip 6 miles, allow 3½ hours
High point 4200 feet, elevation gain 1300 feet
July–October
Sidetrip up Silver Peak 2 miles round trip, allow 2 hours
High point 5603 feet, elevation gain 1400 feet
July–October

Grand trees, a mountain lake, and a mountaintop with great views south over rolling ridges to Rainier, west to the Olympics (Annette Lake directly below your feet), north to Snoqualmie Pass peaks, and east across Keechelus Reservoir to Mount Margaret, so

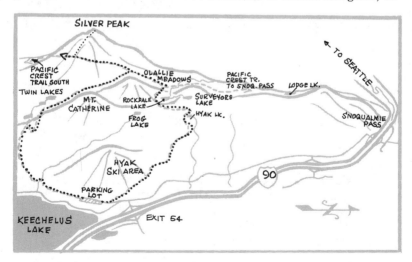

Keechelus Reservoir from Silver Peak

heavily patched by clearcut it looks as if it had a bad case of the mange.

Though much of the old beauty remains, long gone are the challenge and the remoteness that until a quarter-century ago made this one of the most popular hikes near Snoqualmie Pass. This is in the "checkerboard" dating from the Big Steal, the Northern Pacific Land Grant; private landowners cut every tree and obliterate every trail on their sections; despite the problems of managing public lands intermingled with private, the Forest Service sincerely attempts true multiple-use—which means trails. Trails of tears.

Drive I-90 east from Snoqualmie Pass 2 miles and go off on Hyak Exit 54. Turn right, and right again. In 0.4 mile turn left on road No.

9070 and climb 0.4 mile to a junction. Keep straight ahead under a chairlift, ignore spur roads, and follow No. 9070 for 3½ miles from I-90 to Cold Creek trailhead, signed "Twin Lakes," elevation 2900 feet.

(If your sole interest is the ascent of Silver, stay on No. 9070 another 2 miles to where it crosses the Pacific Crest Trail at Olallie Meadows, 4200 feet. Walk the Trail south 1½ miles to Gardner Ridge trail, as noted below.)

Alternating between clearcuts and forest, Silver Peak standing 2300 feet above it all, Cold Creek trail No. 1303 attains lower Twin Lake at about ¾ mile. Here is a junction. Go either direction—the loop has as much uphill one way as the other. We describe it clockwise because that's how we happened to do it.

Cross the outlet stream and grind out 1200 feet in 1¾ miles to the Pacific Crest Trail and turn right (north). For the sidetrip ascent of Silver Peak, in an up-and-down ½ mile watch carefully for the sign marking Gardner Ridge trail, an old route to Hanson Creek. Easy to miss, the sidetrail gains 600 feet in a scant ½ mile that seems a long 1 mile to heather-and-shrub parklands. The mountainside is broken by a large talus; some hikers go straight up the rocks, but skirting them left or right is easier. Above the talus follow the flowery ridge crest, then 200 feet of steep, shattered rock to the 5603-foot summit.

Having returned from the sidetrip ascent to the Pacific Crest Trail, continue northward to road No. 9070 at Olallie Meadows, turn right on it about 400 feet, find trail No. 1348, and follow it 1 mile back to Twin Lakes and so home.

Lodge Lake
(Map—page 206)

Round trip 3 miles, allow 2 hours
High point 3500 feet, elevation gain 500 feet in, 375 feet out
June–November

North of the a-building Snoqualmie Pass City destination resort, the Alpine Lakes Wilderness summons the seeker of peace and green. South of the pass the sensitive hiker quails at the nakedness of ski slopes and clearcuts, the thrusts of overcommunication and chairlift towers, the webs of powerlines and logging roads. So strongly does the north call and the south repel that—ironically—a person may find more solitude to the south. The squalor does yield at last to virgin forests and lonesome lakes. Much history is there too, to be felt if not seen.

Drive I-90 to Snoqualmie Pass. Coming from the west, go off on Exit 52; from the east, on Exit 54. Follow the frontage road on the south side of the freeway to the west edge of the ski area and take a dirt road 0.2 mile to the far end of a large parking area and the Pacific Crest Trail trailhead, elevation 3000 feet.

Walk ¼ mile in forest. Flinch as the trail emerges to groomed slopes of the Summit Ski Area. On a sunny day hope for a cloud because the only shade is that of chairlift towers. But the absence of trees does open grand views of the Alpine Lakes Wilderness. From this distance the ski area warming huts, hotels, and restaurants look sort of like a scene from a Swiss Alpine Calendar. Sort of.

In ¾ mile the way tops a saddle, the 3500-foot high point of the trip, and gently descends to Beaver Lake (pond, really), 3300 feet, a scant 1 mile from the parking lot. The surveyor paused to photograph a great blue heron feeding in the lake. The bird took squawking exception to this invasion of privacy and flapped up in the air, circled around, landed on a tree too skinny to hold its weight, fell off, circled around, and, cursing still, disappeared over the ridge.

The trail continues the descent, at 1½ miles reaching Lodge Lake, 3125 feet. Pristine! Amid the uproar of high-speed juggernauts, heavy

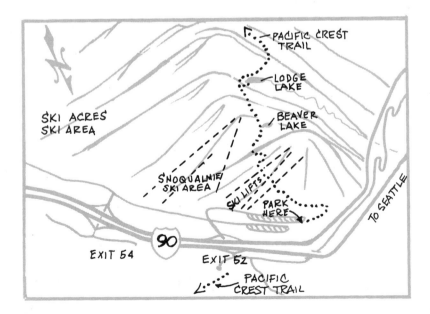

Beaver Lake and Denny Peak, from along the way to Lodge Lake

logging, and mechanized recreation, scarcely changed from 1914. Except the trees have added a few inches. And the lodge has been gone half a century.

The Greenway idea has had many births, in many minds, separately and independently. At this subalpine meadow-marsh ringed by little old trees occurred one of the earliest and most momentous. Here in 1914 The Mountaineers, whose first mountain ascent as a club was Si in 1907, built Snoqualmie Lodge as a base for weekending. Those lucky enough to have a full weekend would take the streetcar to downtown Seattle to catch the Milwaukee train Saturday (or better, Friday after work or school) and get off at Rockdale Station, the west portal of the Snoqualmie Tunnel. By candle lantern the Friday-nighters would climb the short, steep trail, fire up the wood range (the one that in the 1940s burnt the lodge to the ground), and sing-song and hippetty-hop to strains of the accordion. Arise at dawn to climb one or more of the 20 Snoqualmie Lodge Peaks. Back at dusk for more jigging and singing. Up Sunday morning to "grab" another peak, in the friendly race to earn pins. Down the trail to the train in dusk and so home. The Snoqualmie Lodge was the birthplace of weekend climbing in the Northwest; from "pin peaks" was to evolve, in the 1930s, the Climbing Course and a mountaineering tradition the equal of any in America.

The lodge was too much fun to stay home in winter. Ice skating, sledding, and snowball fights led to snowshoe tramps. Scandinavians amused the group with their eccentric snowshoes, not webs but long and skinny boards. The oddity caught on, the Meany Ski Hut was built near Stampede Pass, and the Patrol Race from Snoqualmie Lodge to Meany was a prestigious Northwest competition almost until World War II. Touring (later called "cross-country") was the sport, then. But when Seattle Parks Department rigged a rope tow at the pass, Mountaineers began sneaking the trail from Lodge Lake to "Municipal Hill" for the novelty of gaining elevation without effort. No honor, of course, to those pioneering yo-yos. Honor was reserved for ski-mountaineers who toured from the lodge to Olallie Meadows and beyond to the summit of Silver Peak.

Beyond the Cascade Crest in the Great American Steppe

A *Seattle Times* editorial of July 16, 1992, put Snoqualmie Pass in just if rude perspective:

> *Travelers to or through Snoqualmie Pass are greeted with a panorama that varies moment to moment, mile by mile. Majestic mountain peaks fade into the background as the eye is bombarded, first by downhill ski areas, unlovely sights all but a few months of the year, then by massive clearcuts.*
>
> *More recently roadside developments at the pass—both commercial and residential—have further detracted from the natural grandeur and scenic potential of that unique stretch of interstate highway.*
>
> *Let's face it. Snoqualmie Pass today is, well, tacky. The eastern gateway to the Puget Sound region is a haphazard conglomeration of A-frames and services for travelers and skiers....*
>
> *[T]he Snoqualmie Pass Planning Advisory Council [is] a committee of concerned folks working with planners and consultants to guide development in the pass over the next 20 years.... The plans are consistent with the mountains-to-sound greenway project. SNOPPAC consultants say the property owners "want a pleasant, attractive thing.... The pass could be one of the main focal points of the corridor."*
>
> *It could be but it's not. Today Snoqualmie Pass is more a scenic blight than scenic delight.*

Such is the challenge to Kittitas County (mainly), King County, a possible new municipality, the state, the U.S. Forest Service, and a dozen-odd entrepreneurs who share heirship to the Northern Pacific Land Grant, described by the historian of the West, Bernard DeVoto, as among the grossest gluttonies of "The Great Barbecue."

Snoqualmie Pass is traveled by 20,000 vehicles a day, second in America only to Donner Summit between northern California and Reno. The volume of traffic would seem to bode fairly well for a "year-round destination resort" on the order of Whistler Village in British Columbia and Mount Bachelor in Oregon. Skiing aside (as it often is, due to snow of small volume and poor quality compared to Sun Valley

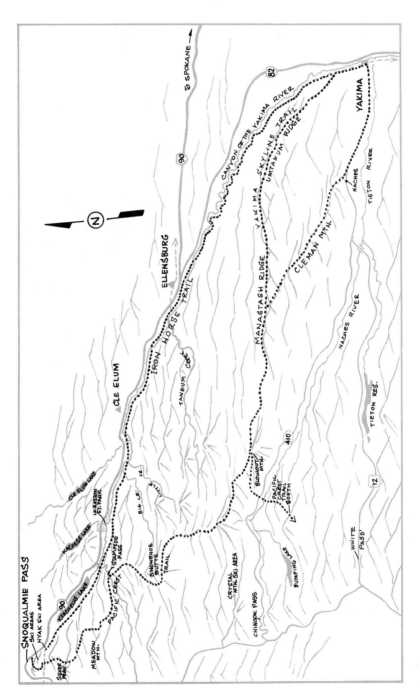

and Aspen) there is thought to be a market for condominiums, houses, chalets, hotels, restaurants, bars, convention centers, shopping malls, and championship 18-hole golf courses.

The Greenway concept is expected (hoped) to have some influence. The Greens already have won a famous victory. Multiple-users sought to de-wild the entire pass vicinity. Denny Mountain and Source Creek and Gold Creek did go the way of all deserving real estate, but Guye–Cave Ridge–Snoqualmie and Commonwealth Basin were saved by the 1976 dedication of the Alpine Lakes Wilderness, which guaranteed that pedestrians always will have a quick escape from destination-resorters—and, as well, from wheels, motor-driven or not.

This book is not a treatise on urban planning and consciously averts its eyes from the fate of Snoqualmie Pass. Also at the pass this book cuts off trail descriptions, leaving the continuing story to other books such as *100 Hikes in Washington's Alpine Lakes* and *100 Hikes in Washington's South Cascades and Olympics*. This pair treats the walking from the upper ("cold") timberline of the Cascade Crest east to the rainshadow side of the range and down to the lower ("dry") timberline where forest yields to sagebrush. Our *55 Hikes in Central Washington* steps out into the sagebrush steppe, the country of the big blue sky, long horizons, sunshine, exciting winds, raptors patrolling on high to spot suppers scurrying through the grass, and flowers that bloom in the spring while Puget Sound remains in the grip of gray wet and mountains in the white death.

Is "greenway" appropriate? Perhaps better, in spring, "rainbow-way"? In fall, when the grass, the leaves of aspen and cottonwood, and the needles of the larch (the evergreen that is not) turn color, "goldenway"?

The Greenway will not stop at the Cascade Crest, will continue eastward, tying together the wet side and the dry side of the mountains. The route (or routes—there need not be a single lane) has not been defined and the pondering is likely to continue. Following is some pondering by the surveyor (for more, see *55 Hikes*).

To tie together the peoples of the cities, towns, and ranches, there must be a Low-Line Greenway. East from Snoqualmie Pass it would follow the Milwaukee/Iron Horse Trail through the Kittitas Valley to Ellensburg. At the Ellensburg junction of two railway grades it would leave the Milwaukee, which there strikes off east, for the Burlington-Northern, which winds through the Yakima River Canyon (the single most awesome act of Nature in Central Washington if we define the Columbia River and all that lava as Eastern Washington) to the Yakima River Greenway.

Yakima River from the Yakima Rim Trail

The surveyor's preference for a High-Line Greenway (Goldenway, Flowerway) is south along the Pacific Crest National Scenic Trail some 20 miles from Yakima Pass to Blowout Mountain. (Along the way the knowledgeable hiker may espy a surviving stretch of the ancient over-the-hump trail of the Original Residents; when protective measures have been taken, its location may be publicly revealed.) At Blowout it would strike off easterly on the series of connected ridges continuous to the Yakima River. In estimated mileages, the way would pass above headwaters of South Fork Taneum Creek and South Fork Manastash Creek to Peak 6290, 12 miles; to 6128-foot Bald, 6 miles; between South Fork Manastash and North Fork Wenas, becoming Manastash Ridge, to a split of ridges, 6 miles; Manastash goes off left, the proposed Greenway route takes Umtanum Ridge right, to Durr Road, 12 miles.

Here, at the crossing of the pioneer toll road–mail road from Yakima to Ellensburg, is the north trailhead of the Yakima Canyon Skyline Trail, greatest steppe walk this side of the ancient Silk Road from China to the Mediterranean. *55 Hikes* lovingly lingers over the 15 miles built by the State Wildlife Department to the south trailhead near Wenas Creek.

Along the way from Blowout Mountain the route passes from the cold timberline to the dry, into the steppe. Everywhere are old wagon roads, newer jeep roads, cattle driveways, game trails. The west-sider who fears a universal turmoil of motorcyles and 4 x 4s and ATVs is surprised to discover so much open space that a pedestrian can spend days and rarely hear exploding hydrocarbons. Establishing a foot-safe path would not be difficult. The route has been traveled afoot and on horse for a century and a half by Europeans, many millennia by the Original Settlers from Asia. Giving a formal name is all that is needed to bring the infantry thronging. The cavalry is already there.

From the south trailhead of the Skyline the way would join the Low-Line on the Burlington-Northern grade, and/or the Yakima River Greenway Trail, for the final 5 miles to Yakima city center.

An alternative (or companion) would diverge at Bald Mountain and follow the crest of Cleman Mountain some 20 miles to near its end, then drop from 4600 feet in about 3 miles to the abandoned Union Pacific rail grade along the Tieton River and thence to the Yakima River Greenway. (Also to be considered is the abandoned Burlington-Northern grade along Cowiche Creek Conservancy, thence to the Yakima River Greenway.)

From Whulge upward through wet-side cedar and hemlock and fir forests to highlands, down through dry-side pines and larches to sagebrush steppe—thus would the Greenway embrace virtually every ecosystem represented in the state.

So brief an afterword as this may leave the impression that the east-of-the-Cascades section of the Greenway is an afterthought, less interesting and significant than from the Whulge to the Cascade Crest. Not so. At every turn in the pine forest and sagebrush steppe are riches of history. Indeed, there illogically seems to be far more history than on the other side of the mountains because in the wet west the works of

Sunflower

man tend on abandonment to moss over instantly and begin melting into the soil; in the dry east the campfires that cooked suppers of hunters-fishers ten or a dozen thousand years ago still yield bone fishhooks and obsidian arrowheads. Trails are everywhere—or to put it another way, the entire steppe is open to the feet, little real need for built trails.

The brevity of this conclusion is simply explained. The tale cannot proceed to the optimum denouement because that might be Independence, Missouri. It doesn't (and needn't) go deeply into history because Yvonne Prater's *Snoqualmie Pass: From Indian Trail to Interstate* says more than our space can afford about the relationship of Original Settlers and Latecomers, cattle ranches and apple orchards, a history closely related to, yet distinctly different from, that of the western beaches and jungled forests.

Neither do we attempt, here, to provide a detailed inventory of the existing and potential pedestrianism. Our *100 Hikes in Washington's Alpine Lakes* takes the hiker's eyes to vistas of the "River of the West" and the three-state vastness of its lava plateau. Our *100 Hikes in Washington's South Cascades and Olympics* leads to overlooks of Wenatchee, Yakima, and the Horse Heaven Hills and across the Columbia River to Oregon. Our *55 Hikes in Central Washington* samples

John Wayne Trail and the Yakima River near Easton

the whole of the steppe along the eastern Cascade front from British Columbia to Oregon, introducing a broad public to scenic and ecological treasures previously known to few except those who live in their midst. The steppe will receive growing attention. There will not be many more trails; boots already can go freely in every direction, built trail rarely needed. However, there will be more routes established, described, and marked to guide newcomers, and there will be more routes that deliberately protect foot travel from motorized intrusion.

Finally, at this writing, the Greenway is barely past infancy. Birthed in Issaquah, its first growth inevitably has been between Seattle and Snoqualmie Pass. The ultimate route eastward beyond the Cascade Crest (Low-Line, High-Line) is under ponderment and remains to be exactly defined. The story is "to be continued."

Index

About the author

Harvey Manning is one of the Pacific Northwest's most influential and outspoken conservationists. His preservation efforts have ranged from protection of the "Issaquah Alps" wilderness near his home in Puget Sound to helping attain national park status for the North Cascades. The author of *Backpacking One Step at a Time*, Manning has introduced legions of future environmentalists to the Northwest wilderness with his *100 Hikes in*™ guidebooks, co-authored with Ira Spring, and his own *Footsore* series.

Other Books

Other books you may enjoy from The Mountaineers:

Washington's Wild Rivers: The Unfinished Work, by Tim McNulty and Pat O'Hara

With beautiful, full-color photographs and vivid prose, the authors explain the place of rivers in the Northwest, and existing systems for protecting them.

The **100 Hikes in**™ Series

Best-selling mountain hiking guides, with fully detailed trail descriptions, directions, maps, and photos:

> **Washington's Alpine Lakes** by Ira Spring, Vicky Spring, Harvey Manning
>
> **Washington's North Cascades: Glacier Peak Region** by Ira Spring, Harvey Manning
>
> **Washington's North Cascades National Park Region** by Ira Spring, Harvey Manning
>
> **Washington's South Cascades and Olympics** by Ira Spring, Harvey Manning
>
> **Inland Northwest** by Rich Landers, Ida Rowe Dolphin

50 Hikes in Mount Rainier National Park by Ira Spring, Harvey Manning

55 Hikes in Central Washington by Ira Spring, Harvey Manning

Field Guide to the Cascades and Olympics, by Stephen Whitney

Describes and beautifully illustrates over 600 species of flora and fauna found in the mountains from Northern California through Southwest British Columbia.

Animal Tracks of the Pacific Northwest, by Chris Stall

Illustrated tracks and information on 40 to 50 animals common to the region. Available in book or poster format.

Mac's Field Guides, by Craig MacGowan & David Sauskojus

Two-sided plastic laminated cards with color drawings, common and scientific names, information on size and habitat:

> Northwest Park/Backyard Birds
>
> Pacific Northwest Wildflowers

Nature Walks in and Around Seattie: All-Season Exploring in Parks, Forests and Wetlands, Whitney.

What to see along specific trails of parks and natural areas in greater Seattle. Written for all ages and walking abilities.

Available from your local bookstore or outdoor store, or from The Mountaineers Books, 1011 SW Klickitat Way, Suite 107, Seattle, WA 98134. Or call for a catalog of over 200 outdoor books: 1-800-553-4453.

The MOUNTAINEERS, founded in 1906, is a nonprofit outdoor activity and conservation club, whose mission is "to explore, study, preserve, and enjoy the natural beauty of the outdoors...." Based in Seattle, Washington, the club is now the third-largest such organization in the United States, with 14,000 members and four branches throughout Washington State.

The Mountaineers sponsors both classes and year-round outdoor activities in the Pacific Northwest, which include hiking, mountain climbing, ski-touring, snowshoeing, bicycling, camping, kayaking and canoeing, nature study, sailing, and adventure travel. The club's conservation division supports environmental causes through educational activities, sponsoring legislation, and presenting informational programs. All club activities are led by skilled, experienced volunteers, who are dedicated to promoting safe and responsible enjoyment and preservation of the outdoors.

The Mountaineers Books, an active, nonprofit publishing program of the club, produces guidebooks, instructional texts, historical works, natural history guides, and works on environmental conservation. All books produced by The Mountaineers are aimed at fulfilling the club's mission.

If you would like to participate in these organized outdoor activities or the club's programs, consider a membership in The Mountaineers. For information and an application, please write or call The Mountaineers, Club Headquarters, 300 Third Avenue West, Seattle, Washington 98119; (206) 284-6310.

Send or call for our catalog of more than 200 outdoor books:
The Mountaineers Books
1011 SW Klickitat Way, Suite 107
Seattle, WA 98134
1-800-553-4453